Shattered Earth:

Approaching Extinction

For my dear friend,

Ian Kra~

January 18 2020

Dr. Ian Prattis

Manor House

Library and Archives Canada Cataloguing in Publication

Title: Shattered earth : approaching extinction / Dr. Ian Prattis.
Names: Prattis, J. I., author.
Identifiers: Canadiana 20190198648 |
ISBN 9781988058511 (hardcover) |
ISBN 9781988058504 (softcover)

Subjects: LCSH: Environmental degradation. | LCSH: Climatic changes. | LCSH: Environmental protection.

Classification: LCC GE140 .P73 2019 | DDC 363.7—dc23

Front Cover art: Yevgen Lagunov / Shutterstock: Fragile Glass World Broken

First Edition.
Cover Design-layout / Interior- layout: Michael Davie
144 pages / 51,665 words. All rights reserved.
Published Oct. 21, 2019 / Copyright 2019
Manor House Publishing Inc.
452 Cottingham Crescent, Ancaster, ON, L9G 3V6
www.manor-house.biz (905) 648-2193

Description: It begins with a futuristic analysis of Climate Change and the inevitable fate provided by the suicide pact engineered by corrupt corporations for most of humanity. From there, the book examines destructive environmental trends and practices and explores ways to protect and preserve planet Earth.

"Each chapter is a shard of Broken Glass. Each one leads us closer to the revelation that we can make a difference in the Climate Crisis if we band together and act now."
- Windy Lynn Harris

This project has been made possible [in part] by the Government of Canada. *« Ce projet a été rendu possible [en partie] grâce au gouvernement du Canada.*

Funded by the Government of Canada
Financé par le gouvernement du Canada | Canadä

For the brave children of our world

ACKNOWLEDGEMENTS

I offer a deep bow of gratitude for the Testimonials for this book. I appreciate the views of each person and am humbled by their trust in my work. Thank you Claudiu Murgan, Barbara White, Jana Begovic, Susan McLennan, Koozma Tarasoff, Rabia Wilcox, Gary Finnan, Rolly Montpellier, Anita Rizvi, Romola V. Thumbadoo, Krystina McGuire-Eggins and Judith Matheson. My thanks also to publisher Michael Davie and Manor House for cover design, Foreword, and publishing-releasing my book to a world audience.

It was quite a stretch for me to travel from being a Professor to a Scribbler! It has certainly been well worth-while as *Redemption* got Gold at the 2015 Florida Book Award and *Trailing Sky Six Feathers* received the 2015 Quill Award. The 2014 Silver for Environment went to *Failsafe: Saving the Earth from Ourselves* from the Living Now Literary Awards. In 2019 *Our World is Burning* received Gold for eLit Excellence Awards. I received the 2011 Ottawa Earth Day Environment Award and in 2018 the Yellow Lotus award from the Vesak Project for spiritual guidance and teaching dharma.

Ottawa Independent Writers have picked up excerpts from this book for anthologies featuring short stories *Love Lost, Dark Shadows* and *The Transfer Particle* while *Sacred Stalker* is now featured in Ariel Chart Literary Journal. I thank respective editors Bob Barclay and Mark Rossi for their belief in my work.

PRAISE FOR *SHATTERED EARTH*

Claudiu Margan, author:

"Ian Prattis's previous books - *Failsafe: Saving the Earth From Ourselves; New Planet New World,* and *Our World is Burning –* should be part of our schools' curriculum. *Shattered Earth* makes no exception. It has an abrasive message for those that still don't want to understand that the existing ecological balance is broken and only a sudden halt of the destructive actions fuelled by greed and power could dim down the effects. A must read for all that care about their legacy."

Barbara A. White, M.A. and Critic:

"I often find myself observing [occasionally out loud in genuine astonishment] that "Ian was right!" He has anticipated all of the major threats to personal fulfillment and global peace and harmony. The path he has long advocated and expands upon in these pages will catch you up in exceptional prose. But brace yourself; there is no going back. You cannot "un-see" the revelations Ian pulls from the deep waters and furtive shadows of emerging global awareness. His wisdom becomes your wisdom AND a fulcrum for your own personal enlightenment and development. Such is the grace and gift of a man who has tapped deep into the well of ancient wisdom intent on saving Earth and humanity. Listen and begin your own healing hero's journey."

Susan McLennan:

"*Shattered Earth* is a glimmer of hope in a very dark time. It's a call to action, a rallying crry that unites all of us in the most epic battle of all: The fight for our survival. Beautifully written and compelling. Dr. Prattis lays out the case for immediate action before it's too late."

Krystina McGuire-Eggins, Therapist:

In *Shattered Earth*, Ian Prattis catapults the reader into a dark, brutal vision of the devastation on Earth as a result of our willful neglect and abuse of its resources. Prattis shares his abundance of knowledge and experience as a professor emeritus of anthropology and religion, scholar, world traveler, spiritual leader and poet, to present a convincing and alarming view of the future, including a glimpse of the year 2080. Using the wisdom he has gained from his travels to overseas ashrams and monasteries, as well as his time spent with Native American medicine people and shamans, he also provides an invaluable insight into the ancient wisdom that can sustain us. This book is dark. It is bone-chilling. It is captivating."

Jana Begovic, Poet, Author, Contributing Editor of *Ariel Chart Literary Journal:*

"In this political and economic climate of climate emergency, Prattis' book *Shattered Earth* reflects Toni Morrison's statement that there is no time for despair, delay, self-pity or fear, but it is time for artists to go to work. And Prattis does just that. His allegiance is to the truth, to our ravaged planet writhing in agony. He paints a bleak portrait of today's reality in which the corporate world uses its unbridled power and wealth to resist and denigrate ruthlessly any environmental movement in order to keep the privileged status quo for itself, regardless of the devastating current and future consequences.

Dr. Prattis is a recipient and bearer of the ancestral wisdom, He shines the light on what is important for our survival, and that of the generations to come, on the urgency with which we ought to act while there is still a glimmer of hope left before it is too late. If humankind wants to survive, it needs to unite in this very late hour, and attempt to reverse the human greed, callousness and cruelty inflicted upon Earth. The powerful, sobering and timely message of this book should be shared far and wide."

Dr. Koozma Tarasoff, Anthropologist:

"Ian Prattis explores earthly society as it struggles to survive the challenges of climate change, militarization, greed from excessive capitalism, and war itself. These are BIG QUESTIONS that even angels fear to tread. Ian as an anthropologist and Zen teacher knows that he must pursue the truth to its end. Bravo, Ian! *Shattered Earth* has a focus on civilization's demise because of the factors mentioned above. Whether humans can prevent this from happening will depend upon their genius. I still believe that there are enough wisdom people in the world that will prevent civilization from collapsing. That is the premise that gives me hope for our future."

Gary Finnan, Author:

"Ian conveys with stark reality how humanity has neglected the basic respect for all that sustains us on our fragile planet. The fact that Greta Thunberg has instigated and championed the Children's Strike for Climate is testament enough to the late hour of the situation. Ian asks the tough questions. Can indigenous wisdom teach us to protect and care for our earth, ourselves and all species before it is too late?"

Rolly Montpellier, Co-Founder Below 2 Degrees:

"Shattered Earth: Approaching Extinction, comes to us at the right time when the era of climate consequences is upon us. We have neglected the warnings of climate scientists and the signs about global warming for decades. But we can no longer silence the truth about the climate crisis. This book asks two fundamental questions: "What is left for us?" and "What are we going to do now?" Dr. Prattis shows how the notion of impermanence will expand our heart and mind to help us navigate through the dark times we will face in our future. The conversation with his nine year old grand-nephew (Chapter 4) is particularly moving and useful. It helped my four grandchildren prepare for their climate-constrained future. I am grateful for the guidance provided by *Shattered Earth: Approaching Extinction."*

Anita Rizvi, Therapist:

"Shattered Earth: Approaching Extinction is humankind peering into a broken mirror and seeing the stark reality of Climate Change Emergency reflected there. Without leniency, Dr. Prattis forewarns of a world with 'no beauty rising from the ashes' should we stay on our present course. Amidst the desolate and barren narrative described so beautifully in this book, a solution is born in the mud pits. Civilization can set a new course that will allow our natural state of interconnectedness to emerge. *Shattered Earth* is brilliant and asks something of each of us - to become part of the only force that can jointly topple the empire of the creators of climate change. With Dr. Prattis there, it is time for the Lotus Revolution."

Judith Matheson, Elder:

"Thanks to my friend Dr. Ian Prattis this book is a true wake up call for us all to link minds and hearts and to honor that this is the "Time of the Sixth Sun" to rise up and to discern the ways of the heart and soul forward. In conversations we can see that what is best inside ourselves is enough to shine light to empower our own deep individual and collective transformation! I hope you all will read this book and see that in this process of touching darkness so to become the light we will all become the individual and collective change we all need to be for our One home to become blessed by our presence."

Romola V. Thumbadoo, PhD, Writer, Coordinator, Circle of All Nations: Elder William Commanda's Legacy Work:

"A prolific writer in these times of unprecedented global and local challenges, Ian Prattis combines his groundedness in spiritual search and meditation, activist peace building and a passionate concern for environmental issues in a search for new horizons in this provocative book. Addressing the complexities of unbridled corporate domination, greed and blindness juxtaposed against the passionate and insistent voice of youth and the cry of nature, he queries the place and potential of ancient Indigenous knowledge in the urgent search for future. In what is now deemed the age of Anthropocene and global connection, can passion and creativity evolve from the seeds of ancient wisdom to ignite a legacy of hope? He invites us all on this journey of soul searching and action."

Rabia Wilcox, Cancer Centre:
"Ian Prattis shows us the dire importance of acknowledging where we are now in regards to climate and the future of our Planet. He captures the true reverence between our relationship within ourselves and our precious Earth."

Table of Contents:

PUBLICATIONS by DR. IAN PRATTIS

* New Directions in Economic Anthropology
* Leadership and Ethics
* Reflections: The Anthropological Muse
* Anthropology at the Edge: Essays on Culture, Symbol and Consciousness
* The Essential Spiral: Ecology and Consciousness After 9/11
* Keeping Dharma Alive. Volumes 1 & 2, Amazon Kindle
* Portals and Passages. Book 1 and Book 2, Amazon Kindle
* Failsafe: Saving The Earth From Ourselves
* Earth My Body, Water My Blood
* Song of Silence
* Redemption
* Trailing Sky Six Feathers: One Man's Journey with His Muse
* New Planet New World
* Our World is Burning; My Views on Mindful Engagement
* Painting with Words; Poetry for a New Era
* Shattered Earth: Approaching Extinction
* 2 CD's and 3 DVD's; 4 films
* 8 Professional Honors, 4 book awards
* 26 Television Classes at Carleton University and on TVO
* 50 articles in Pine Gate – Online Buddhist Journal; 200 articles in newspapers, community magazines, 100 professional articles/chapters/book reviews

Foreword

Author Dr. Ian Prattis opens *Shattered Earth* in the not too distant future with a futuristic analysis of Climate Change and "the inevitable fate provided by the suicide pact engineered by corrupt corporations for most of humanity."

From there, the award-winning writer examines destructive environmental trends and practices and explores ways to protect and preserve planet Earth.

Dr. Prattis employs a skillful blending of fiction, non-fiction and biographical narratives to effectively convey his message in a thought-provoking, reader-engaging manner.

Shattered Earth provides both a big-picture look at our planet's environment in crisis along with a more individualistic-personal perspective, evident in his own experiences shared throughout this book.

This is also particularly evident in my own favorite section of *Shattered Earth*: The enthralling *Part Three – Hello Darkness*, a superbly written collection of fictional short stories, exploring everything from a broken lover's loss of his self-created nurturing relationship-environment and subsequent encounter with a violent ocean environment; to a loner's strong desire to save his natural environment from being destroyed by big developer bulldozers; to an act of arson; to an old man braving an incredibly harsh environment to save the life of a child – small-picture stories of individuals engaged in environmental interaction.

Shattered Earth is a joy to read with an underlying message that we need to treat ourselves, our neighbours and our planet with much more care and concern – if you weren't an environmentalist on starting this book, you will be by the time you finish reading it.

- **Michael B. Davie**, publisher-president, Manor House.

PART ONE – BROKEN GLASS

Broken Glass is a metaphor for the broken cycles of Climate Systems that place humanity in dire straits. Chapter One – A Candid Look at the Future of Planet Earth - is indeed candid, brutal and dark. It begins with a futuristic analysis of Climate Change and the inevitable fate provided by the suicide pact engineered by corrupt corporations for most of humanity. The futuristic view is sent back from the year 2080. It is not an uplifting account, even when it reverts to present time and reveals how unready humanity is to encounter Climate Emergency.

Chapter Two is about The Children and Extinction Rebellion (XR). The essay opens with the Children's Strike for Climate instigated by Greta Thunberg. I admire this magnificent young Swedish woman as she impacts generations and many politicians. Yet, the corporate oligarchy will not budge from their greed and power. They have already bought and sold governments. They will certainly gut the possibility of restraint with respect to Climate Change, thereby dashing the bravery of children worldwide. The emergence of Extinction Rebellion, a global grassroots environmental organization that emulates Gandhi and Martin Luther King's adherence to non-violent protest is a disruption I fully support. Their target is the existing political establishment at the beck and call of corporate cabals.

These global protest movements intend to motivate citizens, parliaments and industry to implement massive measures to ameliorate the impacts of Climate Emergency. However, powerful financial interests, the creators of Climate Change, will not allow their power and control to slip away. They are better organized than us; they control the media and have the wealth to usurp any coalition that threatens their power. This could escalate to the collapse of societies amidst violent revolution.

Chapter One: A Candid Look at the Future of Planet Earth

It is necessary to garner a different view of Climate Emergency on Planet Earth. Let us go forward some years:

Survival Base Alpha: History Report - February 2080

What is left of the population in Australia is being evacuated. The sand storms and volcanic eruptions in the interior plus successive coastal tsunamis bring an end to human occupation there.

Total inundation of Bangladesh, the Netherlands and coastal regions around the Earth are a direct consequence of the collapse of Polar Ice Sheets, plus the violent water surges from typhoons and hurricanes created by Climate Crisis.

Sea levels have increased by seven meters. Such cryogenic events dislocate most of the global population, ushering in plagues and pestilence that eliminate ninety per cent of other species and directly threaten remaining human survival.

The entire planet is overwhelmed with refugee camps and utter desolation. While significant technological innovation – electric cars and trucks – predicted a global shift, corporate carbon enterprises continued to increase production of fossil fuels. They burn ever-increasing billions of metric tons every year, drastically increasing the temperature of the atmosphere. This is a catastrophe for humanity, brought about by industrial lobbyists, liars, the carbon cabal and the governments they own.

The global financial system lurches from one disaster to another throughout the 21st century, ignoring the welfare of populations and the ecological breakdowns caused by the consequences of corporate actions. Not only do financial collapses signal dangerous global watersheds, the world food system also crashes along with the chaos brought in by drastic Climate Crisis.

No corporate leaders emerged to listen to different questions or find different answers.

The anger of the populace turned on the powerful masters of capital and politics. At the extreme end of the violence spectrum, this anger boils over into lynching corporate and political leaders held responsible by eco-militias.

Millions of people die from thirst, starvation and disease.

Death arrives from every pestilence available, some of it created in counter-intelligence labs.

The countless millions who die do not include the many wars waged over scarce resources, particularly water. This causes a cascade of disintegrating eco-systems. Government, industry, banks and financiers grow wealthy while they permit a systematic breakdown of failing ecosystems on Planet Earth.

However, among nations and industry there was also willful disregard and denial of warnings from scientists and oceanographers screaming that eco-systems are disintegrating.

It was no longer an ecological issue, no matter how desperate the predictions are. Rather it is a political/ economic issue brought on by industrialists and politicians who refuse to change and act differently.

This is the picture of a powerful sector whose greedy consumption destroys the natural world. That is humanity's reality while the policies and corporate brand of economics force them off the edge of the cliff.

The consequences are worldwide. Social order breaks down in mid-century ushering in the overthrow of governments, the establishment of martial law and neo-Nazism.

In the vacuum of social order, opportunistic warlords and militias take over many parts of the world - all of which increases the desperation of populations worldwide who take to the streets in mass riots.

Survival Base Alpha: Psychological Report - June 2080

The reaction to crises and breakdown across Planet Earth does not foster adaptation or forward thinking. The velocity of Climate Crisis makes the planet unsustainable for humanity, despite the various accords signed by the international community.

Democracies such as Canada are at the mercy of the powerful carbon-combustion cabal who are unwilling to do anything constructive about this catastrophe for humanity. Democracies, by and large, disintegrated into devastation and anarchy.

China's autocratic and highly centralized government is the only state that could take monumental measures but was riven with internal conflicts. Chinese leaders evacuated the coastal areas and built inland cities to relocate hundreds of millions of people to higher ground but are unable to maintain social order. Their autocratic edicts are resisted by many sectors of the population, even by sections of the army. No other nation had such tight control over their population as China and it breaks down in the face of massive opposition and the accumulating impact of radical Climate Emergency. This outcome in China was predicted in 2014 when Naomi Oreskes and Erik Conway wrote a provocative sci-fi fiction novella titled "The Collapse of Western Civilization." Their radical view of the future was dismissed as speculative fiction. A big mistake.

Homo Sapiens are good at creating problems, which are usually solved in one way or another. But in the 21st century Industrial Growth Civilization, the situation overwhelms problem-solving capabilities. Ecological short sightedness and political greed block scientific common sense.

Human nature becomes defined by symptoms of greed, corruption, fraud and corporate control. This overlooks the history of indigenous cultures that knew how to share, endure and conserve their ecology. They had an inherent view of long-term sustainability characterized by planning seven generations into the future. The global economy does not accept any of these proven historical strategies of thriving. It evolves to gross financial manipulation where powerful corporations collude and morph into an out-of-control monster that fails to sustain the well being of human society and Planet Earth. Sustainability is not in their vocabulary and people become disconnected from one another and from Nature.

Citizens of Planet Earth become dazzled by technological power and rely on someone else's definition of economy and society. That someone else was something else, the carbon cabal, and it does not have their best interests at heart. What evolves during the Industrial Growth Civilization in the 21st century on Planet Earth is a complex web of powerful corporate and government interests that became known as the carbon cabal. It is not just energy industries in oil and gas. It extends into the manufacturing and servicing sectors. Also into mining, pharmaceuticals, high tech and other large scale corporations. All of these are swallowed up by the corrupt financial institutions that run the marketing sectors.

This collective power extends through the media and is successful in making science and ecological concerns into public enemy number one. The extensive regulatory agencies of this cabal have a bottom line for profits only. It is so influential that it stops nations doing anything constructive about Climate Crisis.

This powerful cabal circumvents the Climate Change accords agreed upon by the international community. They effectively discredit scientists blowing the whistle about climate change, so that the necessity of taking early precautions rarely happens.

Billionaire members of the cabal finance effective campaigns to create denial of climate change, paying rogue scientists huge amounts of money to lie to the general public. The cabal is in charge globally, and clearly knows what is happening.

Survival Base Alpha: Prediction - October 2080

Imagine an ancient ecologist on Mars studying a million years of earth history. She would note a parasitic infestation on Planet Earth that was not very intelligent. An intelligent parasite would ensure the good health of the host that supports it. And so the Martian ecologist would factor in an inevitable elimination date for our species in her star-date log and may well view our civilization as a failed genetic experiment.

We may have to accept this musing as a potential reality staring at us from the near future. Our present values and patterns of consumption are the architects of the present global Ecological Emergency. We are, in fact, our environment. It is our collective habits, thoughts and patterns that have created a flimsy, uncertain future for our species.

Every ecology agency on the planet provides dire warnings to humanity about the effects of Climate Crisis. The Climate Emergency is also the symptom and outcome of a maladaptive human mindset. It is clear that our current non-sustainable energy and economic systems are not working. Neither are our minds.

Present Time

Are we too late to chart a Beginning Anew for humanity? Can we engineer a communal Hero's Journey to reconstruct society based on ecology, caring and sharing, while power elites ignore their complicity in the destruction of life on Planet Earth? Let us face it - the Industrial Growth Civilization is a system devouring itself, dislocating the organic structures of Mother Earth to the point that all species, not just our own, are at risk. It has taken us to a dangerous precipice. From there we stare into the abyss of Climate Emergency, ecosystem collapse, ISIL, resource wars, terrorism, white supremacy, permanent refugees and anarchy. Are we at an end game without a philosophy for the future?

How could the human mind capable of monumental achievements neglect the destruction of a lived-in-ecosystem? Our addictive dependence on carbon based energy propelled the downward spiral of devastation on our planet. The process was enabled because we allowed the environment to become an extension of human egocentric needs and values, an ego-sphere rather than an eco-sphere. In this ego-sphere we consume mindlessly in the global economy without regard for ecosystem balance, while creating inequality, poverty and ecosystem imbalance. Planetary care is not part of this agenda.

In the 1980s it was possible to make the leap to a zero-net-carbon world. Yet the opposite trajectory was chosen with a rapid increase in greenhouse gases, as wealthy nations and oil, gas and coal enterprises doubled their production of fossil fuels. We have had the scientific knowledge since 1980 to create the solution, but the obstacles were not technical or scientific. The obstacles are the attitudes, values and concepts that define the dominance of corporate values. Their bottom line of profits was upheld by successive governments that devalued science. It was never about the unanimity of science. It was about the brand of economics favored by the carbon cabal of extraordinary power that held governments in their thrall.

The focus on the bottom line of economic wealth at all costs was very stupid. Big Oil and government created propaganda campaigns to promote oil and gas extraction, irrespective of the damage caused to ecosystems and populations. They produced false images of reforestation, utmost safety, deep concern for wildlife, populations and clean water – and duped most citizens. This played to receptive audiences yet decades later we find rivers and lakes occupying a wasteland.

Oil derivatives swiftly poured through interconnected waterways. Indigenous populations world-wide that once augmented their households with fish, game and forest products are no more. They either relocated or died. This effectively torpedoed any form of transition to a sustainable, renewable economy.

Did anyone notice that degradation of the Earth's ecology was the catalyst for radical Climate Catastrophe? Food crops were destroyed by horrendous heat waves as carbon dioxide poured into the atmosphere. Did no-one realize that food riots and world panic trace back to one cause, the economic agenda of fossil fuel extraction? The undercover deal between governments and fossil extraction corporations was invested in political and economic structures that destabilized world order.

Nathaniel Rich's brilliant essay (NYT Magazine August 5, 2018) shows clearly that there was a decisive possibility – forty years ago - for a turning point. Only it was never taken.

A small group of scientists, politicians and activists in America came to a broad understanding of the causes and dynamics of climate change. Put directly: scientists had realized that the more carbon dioxide in the atmosphere, then the warmer Earth would become. And in doing so it would trigger a violent atmospheric wrecking of the planet.

In 1979 they placed their findings and consensus to the highest levels of government and industry in the United States and around the world. The scientists included James Hansen, NASA climate studies; Gordon MacDonald, geophysicist; Jule Charney, meteorologist; Steve Schneider, environmental biologist; George Woodall, ecologist and many more world class scientists. Politicians such as Al Gore and lobbyist Rafe Pomerance took the scientific findings to the White House and to energy giants such as Exxon. The latter were distinctly uncomfortable about how much they would be blamed for climate change.

Despite their early support, the energy giants quickly turned the dialog to finding mouthpieces that could state that the scientific findings were not translatable into global disasters.

The scientists attempted to divert the catastrophe with a clear grasp of what was causing Climate Crisis. Their lobbying was straightforward from their meticulous scientific findings. Their emphasis to politicians and industry was about the freezing of carbon emissions and the development of alternative energy that did not create carbon dioxide. At that time, some forty years ago, it seemed to be a good idea to many world leaders.

A consensus based plan, however, would not happen without American leadership. The United States was the obvious nation to lead such an outcome. It failed to do so, much to the chagrin and reputation of the scientists, as their findings were censored and belittled. They then became targets that the carbon cabal sought to undermine.

The evidence, however, was drastic. The UN reported that in 1990 more than 20 billion metric tons of carbon dioxide was placed in the atmosphere from fossil fuels. And by 2018 it is in excess of 32.5 billion metric tons, accompanied by the deadly tsunamis, earthquakes, tornadoes, sea level inundations and water surges destroying low lying coastal regions of the planet.

Furthermore, in the summer of 2019, heat records soared in Europe and elsewhere by leaps of 2 degrees higher than previous records. The European heat wave moved north and settled over Greenland, causing massive ice loss. The Danish Meteorological Institute estimated that 10 billion metric tons of ice were lost to the oceans by the July 2019 heat wave. Arctic ice melting can lead to rising sea levels up to seven meters.

It does not stop there. Central Africa and the Arctic Circle are presently surrounded by unprecedented wildfires. That will have a drastic impact on wild animals and the people living in these regions, as well as releasing searing amounts of CO_2 into the atmosphere. Furthermore, the Economist Journal on August 1, 2019 published "Deathwatch for the Amazon," which is collapsing ecologically - a process hastened by Brazil's President. The drastic wildfires in the summer of 2019 were dismissed by President Bolsonaro as being set by NGO's opposing him. There was no evidence. Even worse was the statement that his government lacked the resources to fight the record number of wildfires in the region - home to three million species of plants and animals and one million indigenous people. The Amazon rainforest is a sink for CO_2, as it absorbs over 2 billion tons of CO_2 a year. Now it is a source of CO_2 in the atmosphere that further endangers Indigenous communities. It has been a long war promoted by agribusinesses and the Brazilian government against the indigenous population who have suffered from violent and oppressive treatments in the name of development. The Amazon rainforest acted as a major buffer to Global Warming. That prevention has now been compromised, as rain forest degradation has major impacts for Climate Emergency. The responsibility rests firmly on Brazil's President and his collusion with corporate agribusinesses.

At the end of August 2019 leaders of the G7 – Canada, France, Germany, Italy, Japan, UK and the US – met in Biarritz, France. Their final task was to pledge $22 million to pay for water bombers to put out the wildfires in the rainforest. The Brazilian President ruled out accepting the G7 offer and accused foreign powers of wanting control of the Amazon and treating Brazil as a colony. A childish spat between the presidents of France and Brazil were part of preventing a global contribution to Climate Emergency. Such idiocy prevented a global step forward in the fight against Climate Crisis.

In 2019 Harvard Professor James Anderson asserts that present Earth carbon levels were last found in the Eocene Epoch – 33 million years ago. Due to the present warming in oceans he speculates that the amount of water vapor now in the atmosphere triggers storm systems that are violent to the extreme. This is now amplified by the breaking up of the Ross Ice Shelf, which stabilizes the West Antarctic Ice sheet. It is now melting 10 times faster than average and will soon be unable to block other glaciers. As it weakens, rising sea levels of several meters are to be expected.

The obvious knock-on consequence is to create even more destructive cyclones, tsunamis and tornadoes that will destroy human habitation along with other species. Professor Anderson also notes, somewhat dryly, that while the sea-level rise is irreversible, university administrators still refuse to divest from fossil fuels! They prefer to join executives of the carbon cabal and bought media, which fail to fact-check statements made by politicians and corporate oligarchs.

The creature, which enabled such a catastrophe, is none other than fossil fuel industries supported by successive government regimes. This collusion successfully suppressed science, confused public knowledge with misinformation, and furthermore beefed up the blatant bribery of politicians. The carbon energy cabal funded million dollar disinformation campaigns. They paid select scientists to distort the truth and state that there was an uncertainty factor to the scientific findings of climate crisis – if indeed climate change existed at all!

Oil and gas executives – and their billionaire backers – protected their profits, downplayed scientific conclusions as "uncertain" and deliberately dulled the intelligence of the general public. Their design was to control, delay and block binding climate crisis endeavors. Their pathetic, yet successful, message was to reframe climate crisis as a "dual energy challenge!"

In the spring of 2019 the UN committee on Biodiversity and Environmental Science issued a startling video and report, which showed that one million of the planet's species were facing rapid extinction by humans. The 145 experts were drawn from 50 countries. The 39 page summary places biodiversity alongside Climate Crisis and projects that, without co-operative global action, major biodiversity losses will continue to 2050 and beyond.

Added to this list are – oceanic over-fishing, burning of fossil fuel, land and water pollution and invasive species. Furthermore - three quarters of Earth's land and 85% of crucial wetlands have been lost, making it harder for other species and us to survive. This 2019 report rings an alarm yet indicates that the world can reverse this crisis. The major block to such optimism is that climate denial is the baseline for Republican lawmakers in the US. They are in the pockets and on the boards of the carbon cabal and are unlikely to see any responsibility or reason to co-operate with any global agenda to fix Climate Emergency.

Along with right wing politicians in many nations their divisiveness does not allow constructive contributions to emerge that can stave off the extinction of species. What are lacking in the UN's 2019 report are the practical solutions for government, business and communities to apply to a disintegrating ecology. Alarms do not cut it anymore, particularly as drastic planetary change leaves organisms little time to adapt. And that includes us.

The 2019 UN video and report confirmed the radical views of Elizabeth Kolbert who wrote *The Sixth Extinction* in 2014. The six-mile-wide asteroid that slammed into Earth 66 million years ago upended the global web of life and wiped out the dinosaurs and many other species.

This was the fifth time that events almost eradicated life on Earth. The difference between the five prior extinctions on Planet Earth, and the imminent sixth, is that the present extinction is due to humans as the agents of mass destruction.

Kolbert makes it very clear that the acceleration of the Sixth Extinction is mainly driven by the consequences of CO_2 pouring into the atmosphere. The world is changing faster than species can adapt – and that includes *Homo Sapiens*.

Are we likely to rein in our economic growth, our carbon emissions and toxic pollution? Paul Ehrlich in 2014 wryly states, "In pushing other species to extinction, humanity is busy sawing off the limb on which it perches."

However, Darwin's notion of "Survival of the Fittest" can be replaced by a positive theory of evolution that emphasizes co-operation, interaction and mutual dependence among other life forms. Networking replaces combat! This thread of thought is elaborated in Chapter Three: Impermanence and Extinction.

I do not think the UN in 2019 offered solutions – just alarms, while the world seemingly carries on with life as usual. This is unfortunate, as "life as usual" is no longer an option when the carbon cabal holds all the cards. They continue to promote propaganda to the tune of 200 million dollars per year to bring down the "bogus" climate change agenda – and that includes everything that the UN so carefully delivered in the spring of 2019. The corporate oligarchy is committing genocide on a global scale, as the mass of humanity is facing extinction.

In spite of the provocative UN Video and Report in 2019, the carbon cabal maintains a very long arm.

To keep the bottom line of profits in their favor, they are willing to accept that human civilization would be destroyed in the not so far future. Their organization presently pays selected scientists and climate denial groups to promote the position that the existing evidence on climate change does not support crisis warnings. This is a bought and sold lie. Too many citizens, however, know the lack of truth about the US government, oil and gas companies, industrialists and politicians.

I ponder on Martin Luther King's quote: "The hottest place in Hell is reserved for those who remain neutral in times of great moral conflict."

Chapter Two: The Children and Extinction Rebellion (XR)

In the year of 2018 in Sweden, 15 year old Greta Thunberg sat outside the Swedish parliament with her water bottle, books, snacks and a homemade sign "SCHOOL STRIKE FOR CLIMATE." Every Friday she left her school to do this. She says,

"No-one was interested, so I had to do it myself."

She was not alone for long. A flyer she made stated: You grownups don't give a shit about my future. Sweden's newspapers and reporters soon flocked around her. She still strikes for the Climate every Friday. She spoke at the UN climate talks in Poland and called out world leaders for not being mature enough to tell it like it is.

"Even that burden is left to us children," was part of her address to the global business elite at Davos.

She told the EU to double its climate change reduction targets as this would be its fair share of keeping the planet below the dangerous level of global warming. Greta affirmed her stance with a withering Ted Talk in Stockholm that left nothing behind and earned an ovation from a huge audience. She brought a fresh and fierce face to the environmental movement.

Greta Thunberg was named Swedish Woman of the Year and also nominated for the Nobel Peace Prize. She shared the prestigious Norwegian Fritt Ords Prize for 2019 and promptly donated her prize money to the "People versus Arctic Oil" lawsuit in Norway – to keep fossil fuels in the ground. The People won! She also received the Prix Liberte in France and donated the 25,000 Euro prize to four different organizations for climate justice.

GQ Magazine in 2019 created the Game Changer Award for her. She was on the front cover of TIME magazine and lit a fuse among young people around the world. That fuse has brought the EU to consider further steps to reduce Climate Change in Europe. Thousands of students in Europe and over 1,000 cities world-wide joined her "FridaysForFuture" campaign. Her example came amidst very dangerous warnings about climate change. Thunberg remarked that,

"Change is on the horizon, but to see that change we also have to change."

Thunberg has Asperger's syndrome. She cites her neuronal structures as providing her single pointed dedication to the issue of Climate Change. She quips,

"I see the world kind of black-and-white. Either we go on as a civilization or we don't."

Her achievements and example are so impressive that world leaders laud her with praise – Angela Merkel, Bernie Sanders, Arnold Schwarzenegger to name only a few. Sir David Attenborough, an iconic force for environmentalism, totally backs the world wide school climate strikes and states:

"Outrage is certainly justified."

On May 31, 2019, the Dalai Lama wrote to Greta:

"It is very encouraging to see how you have inspired other young people to join you in speaking out. You are waking people up to the scientific consensus and the urgency to act on it..... you have opened the eyes of the world to the urgency to protect our planet, our only home."

This unusual warrior for Climate Change, now 16 years old, deserves the active attention of every adult in the world. She put out a call for students world-wide to leave their schools on Friday March 15, 2019, to "Strike for Climate," and brought out the determination of 1.6 million young people to force the hand of political change. Her model for this was the Parkland School students in Florida, who walked out of school to protest gun violence.

Greta holds the firm desire for global student strikes to be non-violent, with no hate and no damage. She insists that everyone become educated about the Paris Accords, respecting science and personally minimising their carbon-footprint. She requests children to do their homework about Climate Change, because most adults have yet to do so.

Youth Climate Change US pointed the March 15th Climate Strike right at resistant politicians in American States and the US Congress, demanding that they "decarbonize" the US economy, and furthermore take legislative action to combat the effects of climate change.

The 2,083 Climate Strikes on March 15, 2019, took place in 1,265 countries around the planet. Millions of young people see that their present and future lives on the planet are at stake and they are asking society to strike with them. The former British PM, Theresa May, asserted that the school strikes are "wasting lesson time." Greta's sharp response was,

"Political leaders have wasted 50 years of inaction. And that is slightly worse.."

Good bye Theresa May and your ilk! It is not appropriate to ignore Greta Thunberg, when over 3,000 climate scientists have given their full backing to the strikes.

In Science Magazine (April 2019, Vol 364, Issue 6436), world leading scientists declared that the children's concerns are justified and supported by the best available science. Global scientists also point out that current measures for protecting the climate and biosphere are deeply inadequate. They go on to say:

"......young people understand the situation. We approve and support their demand for rapid and forceful action. We see it as our social, ethical and scholarly responsibility to state in no uncertain terms - Only if humanity acts quickly and resolutely can we limit global warming, halt the ongoing mass extinction of animal and plant species, and preserve the natural basis for food supply and well-being of present and future generations. This is what the young people want to achieve. They deserve our respect and full support."

Despite the efforts of Greta and The Children there is certainly frustration. Arnold Schwarzenegger hosted a climate change summit in Vienna, May 2019. Greta spoke to the gathering of minds. She said,

"The inaction of political leaders and corporations in the face of climate emergency will likely be remembered as a crime against humanity, and those who are aware of the consequences but do nothing, must be held accountable."

From the Intergovernmental Panel on Climate Change (IPCC) report in the spring of 2019 the children climate strikers also have the information that since the 2015 Paris Accords over 33 banks have funneled 1.9 trillion dollars into fossil fuel development. They also know that the billionaire controllers of oil and gas companies are ruthless, greedy and smart. They are aware that the carbon cabal quietly funds the climate denial movement, providing enormous resources through secretive networks of charities which do not disclose funding sources.

This corporate agenda can easily sway public opinion and take over political parties, civil servants and regulators. (July 31, 2019, The Star.) Children around the world are fully aware that by 2030, if changes have not been made, there will be an irreversible chain reaction of disaster beyond human control. Their young lives and hopes will be extinguished.

Penguin Random House released a book of Greta Thunberg's speeches in 2019, titled *"NO-ONE IS TOO SMALL TO MAKE A DIFFERENCE."* She uses her earnings in a similar manner to her prize money – charities and climate organizations are the recipients. She does walk her talk and mobilizes millions of children around the world to demonstrate responsibility for climate crisis. Unfortunately she also receives hate mail and condescending columns in the media from adults who do nothing constructive themselves.

That in itself is a measure of the general indifference to the crisis facing everyone in the world. Politicians juggle with the mantra that carbon taxes are "excellent policy" but "poor politics." The focus of most politicians is more on re-election than the state of the world. It is obvious that politics must change. The 2019 Science Magazine makes it clear to politicians what is required of them:

> "Politicians have the huge responsibility of creating the necessary framework and conditions in a timely manner. Policies are needed to make climate-friendly and sustainable action simple and cost effective, and make climate-damaging action unattractive and expensive. Examples include effective CO_2 prices and regulations, cessation of subsidies for climate-damaging actions and products, efficiency standards, social innovations, and massive directed investment in solutions, such as renewable energy, cross-sector electrification, public transport infrastructure and demand reduction. A socially fair distribution of the costs and benefits of climate action will require deliberate attention, but it is both possible and essential."

This obvious program has a troubling catharsis with how humanity often responds to climate crisis. There has been a general belief that the environment and economy go hand in hand, while at the same time people tend to normalize extreme weather conditions and think of it as a "new normal" that they can adapt to. Actually, they cannot adapt to the "new normal," as that gets worse with each passing year. Residents in the wild fire regions of Canada are pressuring levels of government to introduce steps to decrease the amount of CO_2 going into the atmosphere. However, there is a smaller yet effective minimum change that young people are doing. They do talk to one another and agree to:

1. Consider not having children.
2. Live car free.
3. Take trains not air planes.

4. Switch to a plant based diet. Give up on eating meat, especially beef.

These four steps are high impact strategies in reducing CO2, but rarely promoted by governments, whereas they can be a stepping point to move on to the next stage of creating new frameworks and conditions. The least that adults can do is to adopt these four steps as a daily practice and at the same time press politicians to get to work on the program sculpted by scientists.

Thunberg refuses to fly due to the greenhouse gas emissions created by air travel. She knew that the voices of millions of young people about Climate Emergency were needed at the UN Climate Action Summit convened by UN Secretary-General Antonio Guterres, for September 23, 2019 in New York City, USA. Following that is the Santiago Climate Conference in Chile. Greta had already decided to take a sabbatical year from school to dedicate herself to activism, but needed help to get there.

This is where Team Malizia 2 stepped in and offered to take her across the Atlantic Ocean in their high-tech 60 foot racing boat, based at the Yacht Club of Monaco. They stated that they were honoured to sail Greta to NYC and fully supported the UN's call for young people to revolutionize the world. Their 60 foot sail boat is filled with solar panels and underwater turbines that generate electricity, a zero carbon voyage for Greta and her father, who accompanied her on this journey.

In the US she joined the Friday Climate Strike with young activists in Washington on September 13. Their protest at the White House was a warm up for the large scale climate strike on Friday September 20 in NYC, three days prior to the UN Climate Change Summit. Greta clearly realized that the shattering of our planet is out of control, and wants the world's population to feel the scream of destruction rising up through their bodies. She brings to presidents and corporate elites, who have inordinate power, a small scrap of paper which says,

"Your time is up."

She is absolutely correct, as her small frame simply and directly hits the heart. The sacred feminine is at work, no less.

The NYC Department of Education provided a tremendous boost to the week of action for Global Climate Strikes on Fridays, September 20 to 27. Amnesty was granted to all of its 1.1 million students in NYC to attend the Climate Strikes.

Other cities in North America followed suit. Millions marched in 156 countries on the first day of 5,000 Strikes. The strikes started in the Pacific where island nations are threatened by rising sea levels. Australia followed with almost a million people protesting across the country - led by children who are aware of Australia's prolonged droughts, flash floods, catastrophic bushfires, severe cyclones and heat waves. This turnout quickly spread across Mother Earth. In NYC there was a massive demonstration of 250,000 people, mostly under 25 years. Greta addressed the 800 events in the US:

> "We are not some young people skipping school or some adults who are not going to work. We are a wave of change. We are unstoppable. Climate strikes are a social tipping point as the whole world comes together to save the world."

The organizers leading the strikes called for an end to fossil fuels and the implementation of the 2015 Paris Climate Agreement. They demanded that politicians get behind the science about Climate Crisis and that young activists will hold them responsible to the betrayal of their generation. They are certainly making waves when the secretary-general of OPEC (Organization of Petroleum Exporting Countries) makes a statement that climate activists are the greatest threat to the oil industry going forward.

It is obvious that corporations and governments are not taking the Climate Crisis seriously. Perhaps they believe that nothing will happen in their future. How wrong can they be?

At the UN Climate Change Summit on September 23, 2019, Greta Thunberg and 15 other young people filed a lawsuit, suing major carbon polluters on the grounds that the countries – Argentina, Brazil, France, Germany and Turkey – are violating their rights on children. The lawsuit compels these countries to create binding reductions along with other nations. The lawsuit was filed by the international law firm – Hausfeld, showing that the 16 plaintiffs had dealt with the stifling impacts of climate change. Similar suits have already been made to the US and Australian governments.

The UN Summit fell well below expectations. World leaders made some commitments but they did not deliver what was needed. Many countries declined to revise their present efforts to combat climate change, despite a stark warning from scientists that climate breakdown is accelerating and global efforts must triple.

UN Secretary-General, Antonio Guterres, called for a collective global commitment for net zero carbon release by 2050. His call did not encourage commitment. There was a near complete absence of immediate action while fossil fuel subsidies are expanding along with coal power. New carbon taxes were totally missing and the transition to a zero-carbon future is nowhere to be found. The summit was an abject failure.

Greta Thunberg delivered an angry condemnation of world leaders, pointing out that the generations that have polluted the most have burdened her generation with the extreme impacts of climate change.

> "People are suffering. People are dying. Entire ecosystems are collapsing. We are in the beginning of a mass extinction. And all you talk about is money and fairy tales of eternal economic growth. How dare you! You are failing us. But the young people are starting to understand your betrayal. The eyes of all future generations are upon you. And if you choose to fail us I say we will never forgive you. We will not let you get away with this. Right here, right now is where we draw the line. The world is waking up. And the change is coming, whether you like it or not."

America's President made a brief appearance in the audience. After a few minutes he left and walked in front of where Greta was standing. She was not smiling. Her glare was one of scorn for all corrupt presidents who, as Naomi Klein states – cash in for themselves and foster white supremacy and racism to protect criminally profitable actions for the already wealthy and powerful (*ON FIRE*, 2019). The disappointment of the UN Summit did however galvanize the next Climate Strikes that renewed with stronger vigor – 170 countries and 6,383 events on September 27, 2019.

The Climate Strikes drew over 6.6 million people into world-wide massive protests that spread like wildfire all over the world. Montreal led the way in Canada with a 600,000 strong demonstration followed by 100 events across the country. Greta Thunberg was in Montreal and made a speech, happy to walk behind the banner carried by indigenous children. For Ottawa's Climate Protest I called on every group I knew to protest on Parliament Hill and was astonished to be surrounded by the biggest protest Ottawa had ever encountered. Other organizations came out and aligned with the Children's Strike.

I mused on my book "Failsafe: Saving the Earth from Ourselves" published in 2008. I remember apologizing to my students at Carleton University that my generation had not left a healthy planet for them. I recalled that apology at the Climate Strike, when surrounded by thousands of magnificent children. I was in admiration of their strike, yet emotional and sad that Earth matters had not changed for the better. I noticed that I was not the only grandparent who cried a bit. I was also thinking about the completion of my new book – "Shattered Earth: Approaching Extinction" – to be released at the end of October and decided to dedicate it to the brave children of our world.

In Canada – the citizen rise-up made many politicians running for federal election somewhat uneasy at their lack of a climate change agenda. Climate deniers, in particular Republicans in the US, are beginning to look somewhat obsolete, as the pressure of millions of protesters continues. The next step is to make it so uncomfortable for politicians and corporations, that they will be forced to take immense action. That is the whole point of the world-wide Climate Strikes.

XR: Extinction Rebellion

> "It is impossible to exaggerate the awesome nature of the challenge we face: to determine, within the next few years, whether organized human society can survive in anything like its present form. Global warming is already a prime factor in destroying species at a rate not seen for 65 million years. There is no time to delay changing course radically to avert major catastrophe. The activists of Extinction Rebellion are leading the way in confronting this immense challenge with courage and integrity, an achievement of historic significance that must be amplified with urgency." – Noam Chomsky.

> "Only rebellion will prevent an ecological apocalypse.......mass civil disobedience is essential to force a political response." – George Monbiot, Guardian.

These warnings are severe and shocking. Roger Hallam took them to heart. He brought together 15 researchers and activists to help form Extinction Rebellion, which had the bottom line of massive non-violent civil disobedience. It rested on the traditions of Gandhi and Martin Luther King, forming a plan of action that shook the UK first of all, then the world. XR organizations sprang up worldwide and they had a text to follow.

1. Massive disruption and breaking the law gets attention.

2. Sacrifice is necessary, arrest and jail makes it clear what society is saying.

3. Respect for protesters, public and police does change minds and creates the possibility of negotiation.

To achieve this audacious plan takes millions of people world-wide getting involved with every level of politics and industry, all the time remaining non-violent. This is believed to be strategic, as it brings out the optimal opportunity for police, politicians and corporate giants to cross over the divide. Penguin Books were alert to all of this and quickly released a book – *"This Is Not A Drill."* It went from manuscript to printer in ten days and was issued by Penguin in June 2019. Editor Tom Penn states,

"We thought this is an emergency and we have to react like it is an emergency."

The publisher added,

"Now or never, we need to be radical. We need to rise up. And we need to rebel …..This is a book of truth and action. It has facts to arm you, stories to empower you and pages to rip out alongside instructions on how to rebel – from organizing a road block to facing arrest."

The book offers a toolkit for activists. Extinction Rebellion became the largest organized civil disobedience campaign in UK's history and it went viral around the world. The call that drove them was that the next generation would be destroyed without their immediate action.

The political class world-wide has mostly taken only tepid steps to address the Climate Emergency. Governments, municipalities and cities have been quick to declare Climate Emergencies – but little action ensues. The same applies to the media, who do know who owns them! However, there is clarity from XR. The Climate Emergency is a direct consequence of current political, economic and industrial systems. Citizens are becoming aware that ownership, work and capital must be reconfigured. They are staring into the abyss of global populations which are starving and destitute. Political gas-lighting is the usual and immediate response by the rich and powerful.

Gas-lighting prose sounds like this –

" …our future food supply is sound for many decades ….pensions will always be honoured ….. our economy is stronger than ever …..climate change is a mere blip hindering economic growth.."

And on it goes with desperate and false announcements. These mantras are issued to keep the wheels of capitalism well-oiled and this takes precedence over the backdrop of hurricanes, soaring heat degrees, floods and wild fires. There is an obvious rift between the reality of Climate Emergency and the vested interests of the rich and powerful. It is clear that the vested interests have to be uprooted, changed and perhaps lead to jail time for crimes against humanity!

Make no mistake – there is a drawn out fight between the vested interests of the rich and powerful against the reality of Climate Emergency. That is why XR is so necessary. Right now they are facing the paralysis of governments, particularly in the UK, who refuse to engage with what may soon be irreversible consequences, particularly with the Brexit option. Thankfully XR has opened to "truth telling" while governments are lying, mostly to themselves.

Extinction Rebellion launched the radical non-violent movement on April 15, 2019. Thousands of activists shut down key sites in central London – much to the ire of the Home Secretary! The XR activists soon stepped up into being a global grassroots organization for the environment, no longer only a UK phenomenon. It spread like wild fire all over Europe, also blocking a railway train from moving coal in Australia. New York City Hall was blocked, as was access to the Brooklyn Bridge. A new sense of civil rights rapidly appeared all over the globe. In the UK it took only four days of protests to create a standstill in the British capital, accompanied by thousands of arrests. Heathrow Airport in West London was blocked by youth activists with banners – "Are We The Last Generation?" Similar actions leap-frogged through Europe and with a vengeance went world-wide. It was too important NOT to take to the streets.

XR knew that the first step was to protest existing political establishments which still advocate that climate crisis is a major hindrance to economic growth. The next step is to unravel the direct link between the paralysis of governments with corporate agendas, as this collusion ultimately brings about the collapse of civil society. It is obvious to the rebels that their non-violent opposition is the clear way to prevent their own extinction. That is why they have joined a call for mass participation in civil disobedience. They are totally fed up with political failures and choose to make a difference to stop the next generation from being in the hell of social breakdown. They are determined to participate in effective action, which does entail breaking the law and being arrested. They are committed while there is still time to beat the life-denying system thrust upon them.

George Monbiot, Guardian, goes further –

"It is essential to change everything, to radically shift the balance of power. There are no STOP signs preventing powerful people, industries and government from creating destruction for the sake of power and profit. They seem to have impunity, knowing they cannot be touched by law. This oligarchy lies at the centre of humanity's collapse. XR is determined to change this obvious unbalance for the future of humanity."

Ten years ago a brilliant pushback was made by Polly Higgins, a barrister in Britain. She created a campaign to criminalize "ecocide." This was aimed at the destruction of ecosystems by the carbon cabal and their political lackeys. The legal instrument of "ecoside" has yet to be adopted, though her idea has garnered world-wide momentum to hold corporate executives and governments liable for the damage they do to ecosystems and humanity. The legal work of the ecocide movement operates as a counterpart to the mobilization of XR and Greta Thunberg's Global Youth Strike for Climate. The organizations are highly complementary and combine as strong grassroots movements demanding specific legal changes to protect the Earth for future generations of all species.

Unfortunately, Polly Higgins died from cancer in April 2019. Her strong belief was that such a law would change the world. Her work continues with a vast legal team in many countries. Her everlasting quip will never be forgotten: "I have a choice to protect our Earth, or let it be destroyed."

These are the stakes we all face.

2050 Scenario

A brutal and harrowing scenario emerged in May 2019 from the Breakthrough National Centre for Climate Restoration in Australia, written by David Spratt, Research Director and Ian Dunlop, Club of Rome. Retired Admiral Chris Barrie, who introduces the work, quotes Professor Steffan:

> "It's not a technological or a scientific problem - it is a question of humanity's socio-political values. We need a social tipping point that flips our thinking before we reach a tipping point in the climate system."

Admiral Barrie emphasizes that,

> "Without immediate drastic action our prospects are poor. We must act collectively. We need strong, determined leadership in government, in business and in our communities to ensure a sustainable future for humankind."

The authors take a harder look at Climate Crisis than their scientific colleagues in the UN and IPCC. They state emphatically that the existing climate science projections and policy making are too conservative. Instead they explore a 2050 scenario of extreme severity, and show that accelerating climate impacts pose very large negative consequences for humanity. In a succession of scenarios from 2020 – 2050, the authors lay out a disturbing vision of human life becoming extinct in a horrible manner.

They predict that between 2020 – 2030 there is abject failure to act on the evidence. Keeping global warming below a further 2 degrees centigrade is ignored and locks in at 3 further degrees of global warming. The global heat wave in the summer of 2019 has already increased warming by two degrees and the lock in of 3 degrees looms closer. From 2030 onwards carbon-cycle feedbacks are beyond predictions so that by 2050 the "hothouse Earth" scenario is realized. The interaction of carbon system feedbacks drive the Earth System Climate so that further warming becomes self-sustaining. The jet stream is destabilized, ecosystems collapse and there is nowhere for relocating billions of people. The sheer scale of predicted destruction is beyond any capacity to model. Outright chaos is all that remains due to catastrophic climate emergencies from 2020 – 2050.

Their bottom line is that a zero-emissions industrial system must be built immediately. And this requires a global use of resources akin to a wartime level of response – something like the Marshall Plan after World War 11 or even a global Green New Deal. Both options ignite severe political partisanship around the world. Climate science has shown that current projections will likely bring about a further 3 degrees Celsius – a catastrophic explosion across the globe.

Without radical change, Spratt and Dunlop's scenario is a glimpse of outright chaos creating the end of human civilization and modern society. Naomi Klein argues in her 2019 book – *"On Fire"* – that something like a Green New Deal is a radical change that could transform our economies to meet the Paris Accord protocols.

Spratt and Dunlop call out the scientific reticence of climate scientists for down-playing future climate change. They quote Professor Schellnhuber of the Potsdam Institute who warns in 2018 that,

> "Climate Change is now reaching the end-game, where very soon humanity must choose between taking unprecedented action or accepting that it has been left too late and bear the consequences …..there is a very big risk that we will just end our civilization."

Spratt and Dunlop focus on the high-end unprecedented possibilities rather than assessing probabilities from historic experience to build a 2050 scenario.

Their carefully laid out scenario from 2020 - 2050 includes dreadful impacts upon poor nations and regions becoming completely unviable. Agriculture is non-viable in the subtropics and access to drinkable water is rare. Extreme weather events destroy food production and there is no food or water for the global population. Nations are overwhelmed by endless climate warming and pandemic disease. The social consequences are outright chaos. At present, the world is not prepared for all of this. Yet the world's leaders must wake up to the inevitable. Only then can a massive global mobilization of resources begin.

The next decade can build a zero-emissions industrial system. This requires change akin to the scale of World War 11 emergency mobilization plus the call for a Green New Deal.

Professor Anderson gave a presentation to the Oxford Climate Society on January 24, 2019. He made a firm case for a Marshall Plan style construction of zero carbon dioxide energy supply, plus major electrification to support a zero carbon industrial sector. Without something like this, it will be back to the Pliocene era without humanity on Planet Earth. Spratt and Dunlop note that the national security sector has the capacity to do what Professor Anderson proposes.

Spratt remarks that,

"… a short window of opportunity exists for an emergency- global mobilization of resources, in which the logistical and planning experience of the national security sector could play a valuable role."

I am certainly distressed by the Breakthrough Manifesto of Dunlop and Spratt. Can it be pulled off in reality? - is the first question that arises in my mind. I am aware that the fastest growing source of energy use globally, at present, is oil and gas – with their massive carbon release.

I agree with Tzeporah Berman, adjunct professor and environmentalist, that it is not unusual through history for those in power to be behind civil society.

However, we do have the example of the Marshall Plan in WW 11 and the option of a Green New Deal. For that to climb into the minds of politicians and industrialists to give up their "balance positions" would be a miracle! However, it can happen and enable us to get to the real work for humanity.

I am aware of the main opposition to my views – the industrial cabal that rests on carbon. The corporate cabal and large banks that benefit from fossil fuel expansion have the means and organization to leave politicians, scientists and citizens in a quagmire. This has to be undermined by the determination of XR to expose the incrementalism of the carbon cabal.

At all costs the corporate intention to create new fossil fuel expansions must be stopped, otherwise human life on Planet Earth will be limited.

The corporate cabals and banks are rich, better organized, control the media and are funded much better than we are. So we must intelligently fight back.

The carbon cabal are very smart on playing to the fear of change and lack of security. They deliberately lie and disrupt the findings of scientists.

I work hard to make breakthroughs and have my mind on the Marshall-Plan model or something like it. The scenario provided by Spratt and Dunlop is scary as all hell. It is sparse, right to the point and demanding to all our senses.

Extinction Rebellion must make a breakthrough to civil society with their base in non-violent protest.

On Monday October 7, 2019 the UK foundation of Extinction Rebellion shut down Westminster in Central London, the centre of State functions.

That disruption, and many others that took place all over the UK, emphasised that their intention is to disrupt the State itself. Their mass mobilization spread across the population demanding emergency action about the breakdown caused by Climate Crisis.

Am I a part of this? Do I support it?

Damn Right. Hell YES. There and in Canada.

I choose to Rebel.

Cabinets of Bigotry

Old grey men under false hollow light

talk on in the security of bigotry

and rape our minds.

Ashen unhealthy dullness feeds their greed and power

with mediocrity.

Pale grey men terrified of silence and truth

strike the awareness

lurking deep in the centre of our world.

Under false grey light they linger

to banish kindness and decency

as they talk on, talk on.

These false hollow men under pale grey light

descend to depths of sadistic harm

as they talk on.

No mountains of love to soar their thoughts,

no ocean to salve their fear,

bring them out of posturing.

False twisted men under sick neon lights

talk on in the garbage can of history

and grind the world to dust.

PART TWO – FACING EXTINCTION: MOVING MIND AND HEART

What are we going to do now? Is there a future for our beautiful children and grand-children? The Marshall Plan strategy used after World War 11 required a global effort to implement it. Something similar needs to be applied to Climate Crisis in the 21st century. However, given the nature of political leaders at this time it seems highly unlikely that similar steps will be taken. The denial of Climate Emergency by Presidents in the USA, Brazil and other nations, leaves the world bereft. The massive co-operation required to off-set the accelerating Climate Emergency has not appeared – yet. What is left for us?

There is an ancient and unusual perception that is at the ready in Chapter Three: the notion of Impermanence, which expands the heart and mind so that a culture of kindness and co-operation emerges. Impermanence connotes our true nature of interconnectedness with a constantly changing web of life. Impermanence is not so far away from the modern mindfulness movement, which is a vital link in the chain. I will lay out the origins of Impermanence and apply it to community activism.

I introduce James, my great nephew, and his concern for our Burning World in Chapter Four. Some personal steps are in Chapter Five – Transformation in India.

Chapter Three: Impermanence and Extinction

The point of meditation is to grasp our true nature and accept the inevitability of change.

It is impermanence that enables composure in the face of the difficult possibility of Extinction.

The Buddha was very clear about "Impermanence." His teachings on this foundation spur a radical change. The 12th century Japanese Zen Master Dogen writes, "Impermanence is itself Buddha nature."

For the Buddha, Dogen and countless sages this is not a problem to overcome. It is a path, not an attempt to overcome impermanence. Without this insight, we will not be able to change our mindsets about disruptive political and environmental circumstances.

We rigidly hold on to views of how it once was, only it has already changed – often dangerously so. This lapse is further embedded by humanity's general avoidance to value the planet and other people, undermining the possibility of understanding the sheer necessity of "Impermanence."

However, once we can accept that we have created the present deterioration of the global situation, then and only then can we find insights that bring radical change to our values, habits and mindset. Thich Nhat Hanh adds:

> "It is not impermanence that makes us suffer. What makes us suffer is wanting things to be permanent when they are not."

From the Buddha, Thich Nhat Hanh, all the way to Eckhart Tolle and Mooji, poets, seers and scientists - there is a unanimous point of view.

Dogen, from the 12th century, instructs us to intimately observe cause and effect, especially the condition of impermanence and loss. Then he throws in, "…time is always impermanence."

The bottom line is that concentration on this factor releases us from fear and suffering. I offer a simple four step understanding of impermanence:

1. Things change.
2. Accept the existence of the change.
3. Find your composure about it.
4. Use meditation and the fullness of your heart to continue.

It is very difficult for western culture to accept death and the notion of impermanence. The usual response to both is fear and denial.

We have to re-educate our minds to get past these two obstacles. When we can recognize that our present form of civilization is dying, we will recognize that despair and denial will do us no good.

We need to rely on our practice of mindfulness and community-building to provide a measure of sanity. Martin Luther King devoted most of his time and efforts to build "The Beloved Community" as the strength to break through racism in America.

With spiritual practice and community activism, instead of denial and despair, a space opens in our mind for lucidity and steadiness to propel our species to live differently. When such a community walks with us, fear dissipates and the dreadful despair and suffering recedes.

Such a future on Earth requires a mass awakening of attributes that run counter to the ecology of greed. It requires a candid acceptance that our global civilization in its present form is coming to an end. Such an acceptance of our reality on the planet enables understanding of environmental collapse and Extinction.

Thich Nhat Hanh brings this home to us in a challenging way, making it very clear that any view not based on impermanence is wrong.

He shows how the Buddha provided meditations for his followers so they could recognize that the only thing that follows death is the fruit of our action and thinking, of our speech and of our acts during our lifetime. Specifically, on climate crisis he is very blunt:

> "If we continue to consume unwisely, if we don't care about protecting this wonderful planet... the ecosystem will be destroyed to a large extent and we will need millions of years to start a new civilization. Everything is impermanent.... We are our environment, which is in a process of self-destruction."

The origins of the Climate Crisis can be found in greed, craving, delusion and ignorance, where sanity is crushed by the greed for profit and corporate rules triumph over social responsibility. That sums up our overwhelming retreat into denial.

The Buddha advised a long time ago that we need internal changes in our values, our thinking and our ways of life. This means turning away from a system driven by greed, limitless profits, exploitation and violence against people and the environment. By relying on impermanence we can make changes to our collective systems and choose co-operation and living in harmony with the natural world. That enables humanity to flourish in a better 21st Century.

Understanding impermanence brings clarity to our minds and perhaps we can implement ethics, structures and technology while on this planet.

We have the job of cultivating a new way of living with one another on Earth. This is what Thich Nhat Hanh means in his homily, "Only Love can save us from Climate Change."

We must deliberately cultivate positive ethical attributes in our minds. We have to shine the light of recognition and mindfulness on our suffering, so that we become steady and full of resolve to live differently with a community. We have to shift the tide of negativity, change our mindset and not squander our life.

With templates like the Mindfulness Trainings we consciously choose to nurture patterns of behavior and habits that are wholesome and generous. In other words, we make mindfulness practice our new habit, an internal transformation of consciousness at the core of our being.

I shape all of this into a simple personal mantra for myself - "I refrain from causing harm." I know that by refraining from one thing that causes harm, I then prevent other harmful things from happening. It takes mindfulness to do this and the trainings provide the starting point, a guidance system and a deep well of internal ethics to live by.

My commitment is to actualize these trainings in my life, and in the lives of others, so that impermanence is understood.

To mitigate ecological collapse, the transition from doomed economic and political systems have to change to life sustaining societies based on community activism.

There are many hurdles, as people do not see Climate Emergency for what it is, because they are stuck in their personal suffering. The plight of Mother Earth is beyond their capacity to grasp.

Spiritual practice and community building of some kind are drastically needed in order to prevent being overwhelmed by suffering, despair and fear.

I could go on and on about the terrible things taking place in society, politics and to the planet – and will divert to that in a moment. It is important to refine a system of ethical conduct. I go deeper into meditation to mainly fix myself to be steady and insightful. I register with Mindfulness Trainings, as it brings out all that I would like to see in people around the planet.

The bottom line for me is that awakening and mindfulness are active. Activism, on its own, does not have the inner resources to maintain effective social and planetary transformation.

I know from personal experience that re-training the wild mind is a necessary ingredient to precede activism. Becoming environmental or political is only one part of the gig. It cannot be fully effective until the internal spiritual work is in place.

At present, we are totally out of sync with the earth's resources. The fragile threads of ecosystems around the globe are severely compromised and we are in the position of going down the collective sewer.

Earth is like a giant living cell, all parts are linked symbiotically. Biologist Thomas Lewis created this metaphor with humanity as just one part of a vast system. The reality is that the life support systems of our planet are severely threatened by Climate Crisis.

Our ignorance and neglect are destroying Planet Earth, because we do not know how to respect ourselves, others, and the planet.

We have no alternative but to concentrate on sustainable living, rather than exploiting the spoils of perpetual economic growth.

Profit cannot be the sole reason for commerce. There must be responsibility tied into the equation.

Unfortunately, we have largely discarded our ability to relate to meaningful values such as compassion, planetary care, love and social justice to mention a few castaways.

Unless we radically change, there is no possibility of balance, environmentally or socially.

These issues were examined with great clarity by the awakened mind of the Buddha, 2600 years ago. His teachings are timeless, as relevant to the modern world as when first spoken.

In the modern era Thich Nhat Hanh taught the Five Mindfulness Trainings as a design for living related to modern realities. They are non-sectarian and all spiritual traditions have their equivalent.

The first training is to protect life, to decrease violence in oneself, family and society.

The second training is to practice social justice, generosity and not exploit other beings.

The third is responsible sexual behavior for all people, to protect couples, families and children.

The fourth is the practice of deep listening and loving speech to restore communication and reconciliation.

The fifth is about mindful consumption, which helps us not to bring toxins and poisons into our body, mind or planet.

Expanding Heart and Mind - Community Building and Activism:

I rest on the Hopi Elders' Prophecy in 2000,

"Create your community. Be good to one another. And do not look outside yourself for your leader... See who is there with you and celebrate.... All that we do now must be done in a sacred manner and in celebration. We are the ones we've been waiting for."

59

I believe, from my own experience, that community activism is a vital action for populations around the world. I would say community building and activism are essential actions in our times.

For years I organized a big event in Ottawa City Hall – the annual Friends for Peace Day. This was my job for a decade.

It all started on a bitterly cold winter evening as the Iraq war loomed. I received notice that a Peace Song Circle was happening on Parliament Hill to protest the bombing of Baghdad.

So I went, accompanied by my wife Carolyn, a friend and our dog. No-one else turned up, as it was so cold. I remarked to Carolyn,

"This is a good idea but it needs attention to detail and organization."

She replied, "Let's do it."

So we created the nucleus for Friends for Peace Canada. It quickly grew to a loose coalition of over fifty organizations in the city and we asked them to begin the peace process first of all within themselves, then to the community and out to the world.

Our mandate evolved from peace advocacy to projects on the ground. We gave annual Grants to local organizations making a difference in our city, as well as working with other coalitions in the city for environmental and social justice issues.

We organized five thousand participants at the Song Circle on Parliament Hill in Ottawa, held on a miserably wet, cold spring day in 2003.

A sea of multi-colored umbrellas on a rain swept morning welcomed all those gathered.

As other peace protests joined us and sang "All Within Me Peaceful," the crowd covered the grounds of Canada's seat of government, all meditating at the end in total silence as the rain poured down on our heads.

The pouring rain was strangely welcome, for it symbolized the tears of Iraqi children, my tears, your tears, transformed into hope through singing for peace with one another and experiencing deep stillness with this community on Parliament Hill.

There was a transformation of anger, anguish and violence into a determined clarity to be peaceful and to oppose war. From there we know the wise actions to take.

The projects in the city of Ottawa supported by Friends for Peace include: the Multi-Faith Housing Initiative, the Youth Treatment Centre, Child Haven International, and Peace Camp Ottawa, which brings reconciliation to Palestinian and Israeli teens.

In addition, we supported the Physicians for Global Survival initiative to expand the mandate of the Canadian War Museum to include the creation of a culture of peace.

There were other projects in Africa, India and Nepal.

One planetary care project was the campaign to make the Dumoine River watershed in Quebec a protected conservation park.

Peace Grants were also awarded to rebuild the Galai School in Liberia and the Healing Art Project of Minwaashin Lodge – an aboriginal women's centre in Ottawa.

Orkidstra received several grants to expand their children's orchestra. Other grants were presented to the Dandelion Dance Company and to USC Canada.

Ottawa Friends of Tibet received several Peace Grants for their Tibetan Re-Settlement Project, just to mention a few.

Each year since the relentless rain on Parliament Hill in 2003, the annual Friends for Peace Days have been memorable. We were rained and snowed on for several years on Parliament Hill, thunder and lightning at Alumni Park of Carleton University, before we moved inside to Ottawa City Hall.

We organized differently there, with peace activist and environment booths along the periphery of the hall, a food court at the back, a long set of tables with items for the silent auction and the stage at the north end. The response to this community activism was beyond any expectations.

The yearly event, held in Autumn, became an awesome, diverse, unique Ottawa experience. It was made possible by the generosity of volunteers, supporters and citizens of Ottawa who showed up to have a good time, be educated and inspired.

It created an epicentre of intent and action, intense at times as people were moved to both tears and laughter. The intensity and joy rippled through the diversity, all generations, faiths and cultures in our northern city.

The force of the epicentre roared through the community and activist tables, Muslim families, Asian groups, elders, young folk and volunteers.

The diversity of Ottawa gathers, listens, dances, laughs, cries, and takes home an unforgettable experience of hope and confidence.

Friends for Peace presented Awards to outstanding Canadian citizens who devoted their lives to securing peace, planetary care and social justice.

Our mandate was always solid throughout the day, at the Welcome and Community Tables, the Silent Auction, Connection Centre and Food Court. Citizens left at the end of the day feeling uplifted, confident and connected.

The intent was to create a different form of peaceful expression that appeals to a wide cross section of Canadian citizens who want to create infrastructure in our institutions that value peace and planetary processes.

When I founded Friends for Peace Canada I was making a conscious choice to focus on the local, my home city of Ottawa.

My focus was on mindfulness in schools, city environment, youth at risk and the empowerment of women. I was astonished by the results, more true to say "blown away."

At the local level there was continuity with great women who made sure good things happened. Many of the Award recipients were women. The funds raised from the annual Peace Day were used to issue Grants to organizations in Ottawa.

In particular, we supported youth organizations that burst on to the local scene guided by awesome women.

Orkidstra, founded by my friend Tina Fedeski, provides children from under-served communities with the opportunity to learn a musical instrument and sing in a choir. It is modelled on the El Sistema program, which was so successful in Venezuela for breaking down barriers of poverty and violence.

The philosophy of El Sistema has spread to sixty countries in the world, serving millions of children.

In Ottawa, Orkidstra is creating a quiet social revolution on the backs of children – in a very healthy way.

Tina Fedeski and two friends drew together a marvelous group of music teachers, promoters, volunteers and educators.

There are now 700 children from over 62 cultural and linguistic backgrounds – a huge enrollment beyond the 27 children who started in the program in 2007.

Orkidstra is a social development program giving children in Ottawa a sense of belonging and achievement plus fostering life skills.

Children from low-income and under-served areas receive tuition, instruments and music – provided free of charge. Each child commits to playing in an ensemble.

The program builds community, co-operation, commitment, compassion and self-esteem. This is in the opposite direction of fear, suffering and neglect.

The results have been amazing. <u>All</u> graduates go on to post-secondary education making good the belief that empowering kids builds mature citizens and community.

In the Orkidstra domain there is no sense of separation, only love. They interconnect with integrity, a recipe that makes the entire organization deeply heart-warming.

Similar support was provided to The Dandelion Dance Company, which has a similar structure. This is the creation of Hannah Beach, who brought forth a dozen young women actors, dressed in black to several Friends for Peace Days.

This Ottawa-based youth dance theatre company explores social issues through movement. Their repertoire is driven by the experiences, reflections and passion of young women who range in age from twelve to eighteen.

The themes they dance include children's rights, hunger, authenticity, bullying, drug addiction, stereotypes and inclusiveness.

Their performances of John Marsden's "Prayer for the Twenty First Century" brought the entire audience to their feet applauding their passion for nonviolence and the basic rights for women. The dance alluded to our hope and dreams we want for our society.

The Dandelions provide the means to galvanize parents, friends and volunteers so that good kids are created and excellent citizens emerge.

Peace, Planetary Care and Social Justice are alive and well in our northern city. A Circle of Nations no less.

Friends for Peace had a fantastic run for a decade, then I was side-lined by surgeries for three years and I could clearly see Impermanence working on me!

There is now a two week Peace Festival in Ottawa every September. It has grown in ever increasing concentric circles.

The foundations of mindfulness through the organizations we partnered with have taken root in the annual Peace Festival.

All adhere to some form of our mandate: Peace, Planetary Care and Social Justice.

Concentration on my home city was a primary focus. I was inspired to devote my time and energy to moving things just a little bit, so that good things could begin to happen spontaneously.

I soon discovered, there were many good friends across the city more than happy to make this possible – and take over.

This narrative shows how the strategy of community building and activism in the face of Extinction is necessary. This is what it takes to derail the culture of fear and greed.

To truly embrace impermanence requires an open spiritual practice, co-operative networks and preparation for community activism to invigorate the values that serve humanity.

The required global response to implement some form of the Marshall Plan or the Green New Deal is not likely to appear in time, unless political leaders suddenly become brave and make bold choices to connect rather than separate.

In the looming vacuum, deadly forms of Climate Emergency will certainly crash down all over the planet.

Yet the organization of community building and activism provides local support with a strong view of impermanence.

In my home city of Ottawa, Canada, there are many magnificent networks of solidarity in the city to help and support.

There may well be disaster in our faces, yet there is also solidarity in community activism. Martin Luther King's "Beloved Community" no less.

Chapter Four: Through Nine-Year-Old Eyes

My grand-nephew James was celebrating his birthday, yet felt awful about being nine years old. He wished he could stay five years old forever. When I asked him "Why?" he replied that if he could stay five then the Earth would not explode. His lips quivered and tears welled up in his large brown eyes.

"I am scared it is too late, that there will be nothing to save," he exclaimed with a frightened voice. He dropped the unopened gift in his hand.

He was very upset and so I gently guided him from the hallway of his home to sit with me on the back garden steps where it was quiet.

James said, "I don't want to grow up and live in a world that is burning."

A long silence stretched between us. I wondered what to say. I could not say that everything will be OK. He was much too intelligent for such placebos.

So, I spoke to him about the mindfulness community I created and the deliberate steps taken for planetary care. We simplify, make do with less, share and adapt. An important part of our intent is to create environmental leaders and that includes him.

"Why not become a leader for your generation?" I asked him. He thought about that and asked what else did the community do?

I pointed out that we encourage voluntary simplicity and community ethics as a way of life. We start with the Earth. Our large organic garden produces an abundance of vegetables, apples and flowers that are shared with neighbors and community members.

It is a solace for me to spend time with the Earth, observing bumblebees and butterflies while gardening with assistance from neighborhood children.

I told James that the kids laughed hilariously when they saw that the vegetable plant I had carefully nurtured for months turned out to be a giant weed and not a tomato plant.

At the back of the garden, next to the tall cedar hedge, is a beautiful fountain that murmurs to the abundant flowers, which find their way to the elderly folk living on our crescent.

A solar panel on the roof fuels the hot water system of our home. Everything else is as eco-friendly as we can make it for our fifty-year-old bungalow with a meditation hall in the basement.

This eco-effort has become an example for other friends. They consider how much we are saving and implement something similar.

Our focus is also on mindfulness in schools and city environment, teens at risk and the empowerment of women. I admitted to James that I am amazed by the results. At the local level there were great women who helped make things happen.

"You mean girl power?" asked James incredulously.

"Exactly that, I believe that the present millennium is the century of daughters, not so much as a gender separation thing, but as attributes of a holistic, nurturing presence of mind. That is what mindfulness is all about."

I told James that the idea is to foster a strong group of people in Ottawa to make a difference for the betterment of society and the earth. Women are in the forefront of this endeavor. I explained that they are the heart that holds the living waters, the dynamic epicentre that leads to effective action. That is how we will get things done, creating a different course of action and living.

James was taking it all in, instinctively knowing that changes were needed. I suggested that when enough of us change, then our ideas will be in charge.

I told him about a talk I had given about the consequences of pathological consumption. It pointed out that festive occasions like Christmas provide opportunities for the best and the worst within us to come out and play.

Although compassion and kindness are there, they are often swamped by greed, selfishness and consumer madness. We need to re-assess, to move on from being self-absorbed, greedy and distracted.

"How?" James asked again, as he really wanted to know.

I chose my words very carefully, after we walked slowly round the back garden of his home.

"We must locate in something bigger than ourselves; a humanitarian cause, respecting the earth, making our thinking better, being kinder and more generous. How about examining our habits about gift giving and learn to give in a different way? I no longer buy Christmas gifts, instead present gift certificates such as education for a girl in Afghanistan, micro-loans for female led families, rebuilding forests in Haiti, literacy packages and mosquito nets where needed, support for Habitat for Humanity. Such gifts are bigger than ourselves and create happiness for less fortunate people."

I told James how my grand-children proudly take their Christmas certificates to school, and play it forward with their class and teachers.

One boy on the crescent where I live has received such gifts from me for several years.

For his recent birthday he asked his friends not to give presents, but to bring a donation for the Ottawa Humane Society that looks after hurt animals.

All of his friends brought donations, a splendid sum of two hundred and eighty dollars. They went together to the Humane Society and happily handed their bag of cash to the surprised staff.

Other children in the neighborhood have followed suit.

This resonated with James and he said,

"I can do that with my ice hockey team. My dad is the coach and he would help." He waited for me to continue.

"James, the greatest gift we can give to ourselves and others at this time of global ecological crises is sharing and caring. It involves stepping onto what the Buddhists call the Bodhisattva Path."

James knew that I was a Zen teacher. I explained that a Bodhisattva was a person who stayed in the global mess and did their best to awaken the minds and hearts of people. I firmly stated that it is time for the Bodhisattva-within-us to enter the 21st century as the example for action. It takes training, practice, intelligence and creative vision.

"You mean like Jedi training?" he enquired.

I nodded with a smile and referred briefly to my years of training in ashrams and monasteries in India and France and confided that the real kicker for me was the time spent with indigenous medicine people in the Canadian wilderness.

"So what is the big deal about your talk on consumption?" James then asked.

I replied that it totally dominates our planet, mind and body. I tried to explain how, knowing that James' greatest fear was about the planet's ecological crises. He worried about mining disasters in Brazil and China, wildfires in Canada's Boreal forests, Amazon deforestation, Atlantic hurricanes and the Gulf Oil Spill.

"How do we change the destruction of the planet?" James asked.

I said, "We must come to a stop, locate ourselves in stillness and make different choices by examining our minds and patterns of consuming. We must look at how we actually participate in creating these terrible disasters.

This kind of awareness takes us back to what we do with our minds."

"Just how?" was his one line mantra.

"You can start by making friends with your breath," I said. James looked up at me quizzically. I asked him to stand up and follow my instructions.

"Bring your focus and attention to your in-breath as it comes in, then on your out-breath as it goes out. Really concentrate on the whole length of breath coming in and breath going out. Do this ten times. This kind of focus peels away anxiety, frustration and anger so that you become calm and clear. Try it with me and notice the difference for yourself."

He did so and grinned with agreement. I told James that we do know how to reduce our ecological footprint. We also know that taking care of the earth and the oceans takes care of ourselves. We must begin it now for the future, our tomorrow that is shaped by the actions we take right now. I suggested to James that was enough for him to digest, but he yelled,

"No, I want to hear more."

I could not turn away from his intelligent eagerness. So I mentioned that if rampant consumption remains our deepest desire we will continue to degrade the planet, eventually destroying its ability to harbor life. His fears were correct.

Valentine's Day, Easter, Christmas, Mother's Day and so on are targeted by the captains of industry for optimal retail returns, and mindless consumerism is fuelled to the max.

At Christmas, we're often far removed from remembering the significance of this spiritual celebration.

Endless economic growth, the mantra of modern civilization, provides a promise of expectations without any awareness for the health of the planet or of ourselves. Our current non-sustainable energy and economic systems are subsystems of a global ecology that is disintegrating before our very eyes.

We must simplify, make do with less and change, or the burning world will definitely occur. I continued,

> "Did you know that we also harm our bodies through the food we eat, and that it has disastrous consequences for our connection to all living beings?" He did not, yet his mind was a sponge soaking up every word. I continued "The vast consumption of meat and alcohol creates an excessive ecological footprint. Industrial animal agriculture is not really farming. Animals are treated solely as economic commodities and subjected to horrible cruelty. The stress, despair and anger generated in the animals are the energies we consume when they end up on our plate."

"That is so gross," James remarked.

I told James that we can change our minds and patterns of food consumption. We re-educate and retrain ourselves mentally through meditation, choosing to support our body and planet by shifting ingrained habits.

It takes training but we can begin to step more lightly on the planet. It means reducing as much as possible the violence, destruction and suffering brought to living creatures and to the planet.

Bringing peace into our own biological system and consciousness inevitably brings it to all the other systems that we engage with through our thoughts, speech and actions.

"Is this your Buddhism?" James then asked.

I smiled before speaking, "The Buddha was very smart. He taught that the world is always burning, but burning with the fires of greed, anger and foolishness. His advice was simple; drop such dangers as soon as possible. The Buddha taught that it was the unskillful speech, selfish feelings, negative mental formations, wrong perceptions and bad-ass consciousness that burned the world."

James asked, "Did the Buddha really use the term bad-ass?"

I said, "The Buddha did not say "bad-ass"- that was my embellishment."

Then I pointed out that the Hopi also referred to the burning as a state of imbalance known as *Koyaanisqatsi*.

We are not the first generation to experience this. The difference today is that without our commitment to wise intervention about climate change, we could be the last.

"Is climate change our basic problem then?" he asked.

I paused for a moment before replying. "The basic issue is whether we can adapt to climate change. You know about the 2015 Paris Accord on Climate Change as we talked about it before." James nodded.

"It was an exceptional step by the international community, showing their determination to prevent global temperatures from rising a further 1.5 degrees. The signatories returned to their respective countries to "Change Climate Change." What was missing from all the deliberations and press releases was a candid recognition of the "Cascade Effect," a notion from ecological science. Tipping points in sea level rise and temperature connect to tipping points in air pollution, which connect to tipping points in polar ice melt, hurricanes and forest wildfires. All of these triggers create further tipping points that create deforestation, floods, desertification and so on in a relentless cascade."

I reminded him of the wildfires in British Columbia and California, pointing out that the entire boreal forest in Canada is a tinder box due to climate change.

He got the reality that it is not about a reversal of climate change but about learning how to adapt to the consequences of climate change.

I paused and stood up from the steps and walked in a semi-circle before stopping in front of James. In a serious tone I said,

"The disasters all over the world interconnect. Whether it is wildfires, floods, landslides, volcanic eruptions, hurricanes, tsunamis or millions of aquatic creatures dead on beaches - it is all connected. The media and news reporters cast science to the wind when they report the drama and hype of terrible things happening world-wide. They rarely tell the truth that this is another manifestation of climate change. News programs often focus on ratings and openly promote corporate interests that contribute to these interconnected disasters. The general public, by and large, are not educated by the media about the terrible disasters happening on our planet. The other obstacles that prevent the general public from taking wise action are a mixture of fear, despair, laziness, disempowerment and a sense of hopelessness."

There was a silence for a few minutes before I took the conversation further,

"What on earth can I do to make a difference is a phrase muttered all over the world in countless languages. It is then followed by why should I do anything? There is certainly global awareness, but also fear about our future place on the planet."

I then looked directly at James,

"Maybe this is why you want to stay five years old forever. The difficult thing for you, for anyone, to grasp is that we are the primary cause. People *are* aware, but just feel helpless in the face of Climate Change. So what are we to do?"

James shrugged in exasperation.

"Here's the thing." I said, "In terms of action, we have clear data-based evidence that we must cut back, make-do with less and implement a lifestyle of voluntary simplicity. So, where do we start? Of course we must think globally and be aware of the bigger picture despite fear and disempowerment. But we can also act locally in our families and communities. Our intentions then spread like ripples from a pebble dropped in still water. We can hold officials, politicians and corporate culture to account. We can tell the politicians and corporate decision makers that we, as voters and consumers, are deeply concerned about the planet and our impact on it."

I continued speaking on a personal note,

"James, the challenge for me is to be *in* society, but as a *still island of mindfulness*. Take small steps at first, then larger ones. We just need to make essential changes in energy use, diet, language, media and outreach. Voluntary Simplicity is a good starting place. It means making deliberate choices about how we spend time and money. We can support environmental causes with the excess clutter in the basement and always think about whether we really "need" to buy something more. Enjoy being simple and living modestly by shifting our perceptions just a little bit. If we look deeply into what we do with time, money, clutter and our choices, *then we can change.* Notice whether the consequences are peace and happiness for you. To avoid drastic outcomes, it is wise to take training very, very seriously. This helps to avoid all the negative stuff I have told you about"

"Wow," exclaimed James. "OK, I get it about training but what does that look like?"

I was relieved by his intelligent question but hesitant to talk to him about what I was thinking.

He watched me closely and said, "Just lay it out for me." I then proceeded to talk about "Gardening in the Mind." I offered him eight simple steps to refine the mind and then engage differently with the world.

1. You – learn to be silent and quiet! Clear time and space for meditation at home and throughout your daily schedule.

2. Create a stress reduction menu and subtract the "weeds" – the negative energies - in the garden of your mind.

3. Be determined to meditate daily – do the weeding.

4. Focus on and soften your heart – do not be mean - cultivate the soil of your mind's garden.

5. Cultivate the seeds of mindfulness – Love, Compassion, Joy, Equanimity and promote them at home, school, work and in solitude.

6. Simplify, make do with less, de-clutter your mind and home.

7. Taste the fruits of your spiritual practice that change your mind.

8. With all of this you can better engage with the world.

James was entering all of this down on his tablet as I continued to talk.

"Our ways of living together, caring for environmental, political and economic realms need to be re-constructed."

I assured James that,

"Gardening in the Mind" has the capacity to transform how we think and how to cultivate mindfulness. "Finding stillness and inner silence is a necessary first step. We have to find a way to create the conditions for this to happen. In our modern world of fast paced lifestyles there are so many distractions that make us outwardly dependant and un-centered. We also find it easier to close down rather than open up our hearts. But the remedy is within reach. We can unravel the knots of suffering and move from being mindless to being mindful. This is achieved by gardening in the mind. The eight point menu helps."

I paused for a while to find the words to bring my conversation with James to an end.

"James, why do you think we should do this stuff? Here's why. When you are open and receptive you become an inspiration for others. Also, when you can learn about pain, face to face with what hurts, breathing in and out you feel the sting recede as you calm. If you start to close down just ask yourself, "Do I really want to take a pass on happiness?" Remember this - always let go once you feel you are closing down or clinging."

Then I said to him,

"You know what? I have a fridge magnet at home with the words - LET GO OR BE DRAGGED? I see it every day and I take that message to heart. It is essential to learn to be silent, to stop clinging and to find the way to be present in the moment. As the Hopi advise us, never take anything personally and look around to see who is with you. Doing these things helps the world to change. Such a destination is well worth your effort don't you think?"

James nodded his agreement. I assured James that we are equal to the task and I chose not to hold back anything from him during this long conversation on his birthday.

He is an unusually bright boy, as he asked questions and demanded clarification. Yet I knew he had grasped what I had said.

He came up to me as I was leaving and whispered in my ear that my chat with him was his best birthday present ever.

Shattered Earth – Approaching Extinction / Dr. Ian Prattis

Chapter Five: Transformation in India

I was invited to India for guru training by *Rishi Prabhakar* after meeting with him several times in Canada. He seemed to recognize something in me that I certainly did not.

This adventure provided a new territory for me with a number of tumultuous twists and turns.

I traveled to India in 1996 to teach and train in *Siddha Samadhi Yoga*.

The *Vedic* tradition I was studying was ecumenical in character – drawn from the teachings of *Ramana Maharsi* - a wisdom tradition totally relevant to the modern day of climate crisis.

By November of 1996 I had become seriously ill in India. As I observed my bodily systems crashing one by one I knew there was a distinct possibility of death. To this day I am still amazed by my calmness and lack of fear.

"We are so happy Ian that you have decided to die with us in India. And we will be most happy should you live."

Huddled on a bed in an ashram in Mumbai, India, I opened my eyes to see a visiting Swami sitting beside me. He sat me up and made some tea with herbs.

The ashram was reserved for saints and holy men, though I did not qualify for either category.

Lying close to death, the lack of fear provided a sense of freedom and strength.

I felt very peaceful, no longer a maverick standing alone. I felt very calm about letting go of my bodily existence.

My wife Carolyn and I kept diaries about my illness.

CAROLYN'S VOICE FROM OTTAWA, CANADA:

December 10, 1996:

There was a strange voice mail on my telephone answering machine – I didn't recognize the voice and couldn't make out what the person was saying. Was it Ian calling from India? If so, it was a really bad connection.

December 12, 1996:

Ian called. He had left the message, but it wasn't a bad connection. He is so sick that he can hardly talk and his voice is unrecognizable. A cold chill ran down my spine. He says he's had surgery and that his systems are all crashing, one by one. But he's not afraid – I believe he is not afraid of dying if that is what's happening.

What can I do? My first instinct is to go to India – to be with him – to care for him, but no, he says this is a journey he must go through alone. I am so worried. All I can do is surround him with light and love. And I pray – I pray that God will care for him, make him well and keep him safe.

Dad is in the hospital dying from heart disease – two open-heart surgeries in the last month. The doctors are amazed that he is still living. I wonder if he is afraid to die. I'm being forced to look at death, my fears and my attachments. I cry. Dad has been ill for many years and I know he will not likely survive this ordeal, but Ian? Ian is too young. His life work is not done. He still has so much to offer.

Ian speaks about his feelings and the possibility of death with such calm. He's not afraid, but I am. I don't want to lose him. I am not prepared to let him go. Ian teaches me about no birth and no death, that we continue living in all that we touch - simply a different manifestation than our physical bodies.

But this is too difficult for me to accept at the moment. I am attached. I do not want to let go.

Ian directs me to the teachings on impermanence, and encourages me to meditate on the Five Remembrances – being of the nature to grow old, the nature to become ill, the nature to die, the nature for all things to change and knowing that we will be separated from those we hold dear and that our only true possessions are the consequences of our actions.

Christmas Day, 1996:

Ian called. He sounds a little better but is still very weak. I shed tears of relief. I continue to surround Ian with light and love.

And I pray. I pray that God will keep him in his Grace – give him the strength and will to overcome his illness.

Hope is fading for my Dad. He's in intensive care and only Mom is allowed to visit with him for a few minutes at a time.

None of his children are permitted to see him. I pray that he doesn't suffer for too long. I pray that he can find the same kind of peace and calm that Ian has found.

I am terrified that my Dad might be afraid to die. But I don't know his thoughts or feelings and my family won't talk about death. Mom is adamant that I not talk to Dad about death in any sense whatsoever. I am caught in a paradigm – praying for my Dad to let go, to end his suffering – but afraid for my dad that he might be dying in fear. That bothers me so much.

At the same time, I pray for Ian to survive, but my fear is for myself at the thought of Ian passing away and leaving me.

He seems so prepared and accepting of death. Here I am, afraid for my father at the thought of him passing away, yet afraid for myself at the thought of Ian passing away.

August, 1997:

After ten long months in the Heart Institute my Dad passed away. I've come to realize that he was not afraid. He hung on for so long to allow my Mom and my siblings the time to accept his death, time to let him go. I am so grateful that he wasn't afraid to die.

At the same time Ian returned from India and I am grateful to have him back home – alive and well. His experiences in India have totally transformed him. His near death experience also transformed me, for he guided me to look deeply into the realm of birth and death, to accept death, to let go and to see the continuation of loved ones in all aspects of life, from a flower blooming to a family member smiling.

I do see my Dad every day in different manifestations of life. I am so very grateful.

Ian Prattis: MY DIARY ENTRY, DECEMBER 20, 1996

Prem Kutir Ashram, Mumbai, India

Feel weaker than ever this morning. Could hardly make it from my bed to the bathroom. Hope the saints who have passed through this little ashram are casting a protective eye over me.

Perhaps they can cheer up Chotolal, the Nepali cook here, who has become quite anxious, especially as I have not had the energy or inclination to eat the special dishes he prepares. He is watching me write in my diary, so I will change hands and write with my left hand so he can laugh and feel less anxious about me. It worked!

Why have I become so ill? All my bodily systems have gone off line. Is there some major purification going on in my body, is there something I do not see? What lessons are there? Or are my days drawing to a close in the silence of this ashram?

My blood tests from the hospital show that I am low and deficient in just about every category and the medications only make me feel worse.

So many questions and worries yet they do not seem totally important. I ask them then they fade away. It is a bit strange. A few days ago I collapsed and passed out while at dinner at Madhuma's house. I know that she and her family would take me in, yet this saint's refuge is where I feel most comfortable right now. The quiet and simplicity of the place speaks to me. I guess it allows me to prepare for death.

It was not easy to communicate this to Carolyn but I do believe she understands. My prayer is that she does not suffer unduly. Have sent Chotolal to buy some cards and stamps for me. The cards are beautifully hand painted on pipal leaves with pictures of the Buddha, Krishna dancing and other such scenes.

I want to make sure I finish my Christmas list. Sending Christmas cards to friends and loved ones. Feel such a calm about all this that would normally surprise the heck out of me. The calm is just there, sitting with me, just fine.

I know there is a distinct possibility I may not live beyond Christmas and want to send out a Christmas message from India: "Blessings and Love from Ian." Writing the cards has exhausted me, but I feel satisfied and full, mission accomplished. Chotolal brought in a package of mail from Canada: letters and cards from family and friends, a framed photograph of Carolyn, my dearest friend and companion. Made me very happy, also made me cry as I thought of friends I may not see again. Yet they were strange tears, not full of sorrow or anything, just tears as I thought of loving friends.

I keep falling asleep very quietly then waking up very quietly. Sleep is like a light breeze that seems to visit now and then.

I ate a little bit of dinner to allay Chotolal's anxiety, but it is my supply of rice malt and vitamin C that is keeping me going. Chotolal placed some fruit and water on the table by my bed, then left to spend the next day with Nepali friends in another part of the city, taking my pile of Christmas cards to post.

I am enjoying the silence and solitude, now that he has left. It is about nine o'clock in the evening and I am drifting off to sleep on gentle wings.

DIARY ENTRY, DECEMBER 21, 1996

Prem Kutir Ashram, Mumbai, India

Waking up was easy, getting up was a struggle but did that in stages. The quiet and silence inside the ashram is quite palpable and almost visible.

I remembered my shamanic training with White Eagle Woman. Had a dream about her during the night, but do not recall all the details.

do remember that she told me to construct a mental medicine wheel around me and include all my spiritual ancestors. Did that and feel an incredible constellation of energies, like millions of guardian angels from everywhere.

Took some fruit and returned to my book of meditations and began to read slowly, stopping frequently to close my eyes and feel the words.

Have no sense of time or space today, as each meditation seems to move me with its own measure and carry me along.

Feel such a deepening in my heart, all the way inside my body. Aware that there is no fear or panic, just a simple and happy acceptance. That is all that is there. I have never experienced anything like this.

Have no thought of anything and feel deeply content for no apparent reason. Is this surrender? Peace with God? No flashing lights, visitations or visions, only a quiet surrender and being with the inevitability of it all, whatever "THAT" is.

DIARY ENTRY, DECEMBER 22, 1996

Prem Kutir Ashram, Mumbai, India

I woke up this morning, heard two crows saying hello from the tree outside the window. Feel so happy to be alive.

Chotolal is singing in the kitchen and rattling his pots and pans, so I will celebrate this new day with a little breakfast. That will make us both very happy.

Clear insight that this "death" is a spiritual one, as is the "rebirth." I feel completely new this morning, as though I have been rewired and plugged into sockets with a bigger voltage - preparation to continue moving along the path of understanding.

In my family and culture there is very little discussion about death and dying, though as a child I did have an intuitive understanding.

When my grandfather died I felt him as a tangible presence when he was in his coffin. I quietly whispered to this gracious being: "Go to Heaven now grandpa." I also remember at his wake how upset I became by my relatives drinking, arguing and being disrespectful to one another.

In tears, I sought out my grandmother and complained that everyone was making it hard for my grandpa to go to Heaven.

She listened carefully to me and wiped my tears away, then walked into the living room of her house and with quiet authority asked everyone to go home.

It was much later in life, once I was exposed to Buddhist teachings on death and dying, that I realized I was not such a crazy kid after all. I had cared for my grandfather's consciousness after his physical death.

I intuited that preparation for death was also training for life, though I did not always pay attention to this insight.

I was intrigued by the opportunity for liberation at the time of death, though could see clearly that my ego and habits were obstacles in the way.

I did want to be able to merge my consciousness at the time of death with what the Sufis call "the great magnificence," or if I got confused and fearful at the time of death, to receive guidance to do so.

I felt that if my death was aware, then in the final state of *becoming,* my consciousness would take a form that would serve Mother Earth and all sentient beings.

I liked the idea of recycling, it appeals to the ecologist within me.

This retraining, however, was done fitfully, not in a consistent manner until just before I left for India. There, the preparation became a daily practice of being aware of universal consciousness totally prepared to merge with my pitifully weak and not-so-awakened-mind.

My leap of faith was that these understandings about death and dying were all in my mind. This meant that I could use my mind to take steps to prepare for that final moment of merging with the wisdom mind of the universe and perhaps do this while I was alive. Perhaps the "alive" bit is the whole point.

While in India I also trained in the mastery of *"bija"* mantra. *Bija* means "seed" and the seed mantras are powerful instruments of transformation.

The major mantra I trained with was the *Gayatri Mantra,* the main feature of the *Sandhya–Upasana* ceremony - a sacred ritual for *Brahmanic* definitions within Hinduism. It was part of my training in becoming a guru.

The *Gayatri* is considered by Indian sages to be **the** most powerful mantra of purification and transformation, as it expands consciousness in multiple directions.

The successive sounds of the Sanskrit syllables move the individual chanting it into elevated states of spiritual experience. As an invocation for enlightenment it has the effect of drawing other individuals into the same state. This is the theory – as told to me in India.

Two twenty-eight day training periods, six months apart, were the high points that the rest of my training built up to.

My cultural and religious background was not the same as my two cohorts, yet the experiences we shared were remarkably similar.

I could observe my mental states, compare them with reports from my peers then verify them with the *Swami* overseeing the training. Then from my experience, I could verify – or not - the claims made about the *Gayatri* mantra.

The *Gayatri* ceremony was conducted at sunrise and sunset each day. The mantra was the central component of a long Sanskrit chant that prepared each one of us to experience the full effects of *Gayatri*.

Prior to the training retreats I had months of preparation - with attention to specific meditations, dietary regime and sexual abstinence.

I learned how to chant the *Gayatri* and co-ordinate it with the four components of breath: inhalation, holding the air inside, exhalation, holding the emptiness.

There was also a mathematical precision in tone, pitch and resonance of the mantra, as it was exactly co-ordinated with the different components of breath and hand movements over my body. It was complex and overwhelming.

I frequently wondered if I would ever get it right. I benefited from the persistence and encouragement of my cohorts who were determined that I not be left behind.

I also had skilled and patient teachers who made the effort to transmit this oral tradition, thousands of years old, to a westerner not used to this form of education.

Our preparation for each ceremony was through extensive *pranayama* – breathing exercises – before sunrise and sunset.

Attention was always brought to the union of the individual with the Universal.

The rituals of the *Gayatri* ceremony had to be performed with grace. Clumsiness was frowned upon.

I certainly drew a lot of frowns from the *Swami* and *Rishi* who oversaw the training, however the effects were far reaching.

During the first training period the twice-daily recitation brought on heavy night-time fevers.

I would feel perfectly fine during the day, yet at night it felt as though I was running a high fever, although there was no unusual increase in temperature.

I found that my peers were feeling similar discomfort, though nobody was ill.

I asked the *Swami* about this. He indicated that we were all feeling the initial effects of the *Gayatri Sandhya*. Before it could penetrate our being and expand consciousness there was a great deal of "dross" to burn off – hence the fever-like states. I reported back to everyone's relief.

My consultations with the *Swami* became quite an amusing ritual, as members of my cohort would not ask questions. Yet they encouraged me to do so and gave me questions of their own.

It became a way to check my experience with that of others, and then seek verification from the *Swami,* who had quite a benevolent attitude towards me.

My fellow trainees would wait for the results of my consultations, crowd round and listen to whatever I had to report.

We would then discuss it from the perspective of our own experiences. It was amazing at how similar they were.

I felt it wise to always give my experiences last, so as not to provide an influence or "track" for others' reporting.

The most significant cognitive changes came about when chanting the *Gayatri* with the different phases of breath and levels of mantra.

These combinations produced hyper-lucidity and sharpness. This sharpness was essential for me, because there was so much to co-ordinate at different levels.

I felt very alert, as though I was climbing stairs of consciousness.

I was moving through states of consciousness to different levels of cognition but always felt a sense of being aware of where I was, of what was taking place in the multiple levels of consciousness experienced.

New spaces were opening up in my mind and heart, while I was also very aware of being located in the physical realm - an insight confirmed by the *Swami* without my asking.

Not all members of my cohort experienced this aspect of dual consciousness.

The *Swami* was on the lookout for trainees who got "stuck" and had difficulty returning.

He also confided that he had fully expected me to be the one he had to look out for the most and was pleased that this was not so.

The second training period was with a different cohort in a different part of India – Karnataka as opposed to Andra Pradesh.

My new cohort was made up of experienced meditation teachers and exceptional gurus – quite a line-up of wisdom.

With this powerful group of beings the sunset ceremony was conducted by running water to deepen the silence, stillness and penetration of the mantra.

The chanting of the *Gayatri* took place with all of us standing up to our waists in the water.

When it came to the point of suspending thought and allowing the *Gayatri* to arise spontaneously, to my total astonishment it did just that.

At the same time, I could feel and identify the particles of mud between my toes, see minute electrons in the air and look down on my wisdom companions from a great height.

I felt encompassed by the evening sky and at the same time I encompassed the sunset, the evening sky and everything beyond it. This experience was repeated with varying intensity during every sunset rendition of the *Gayatri-Sandhya*.

I never felt it necessary to communicate this to the *Swami* or to members of my second cohort.

I went into total silence during the last few weeks and do not recall talking to anyone, as everyone very carefully left me in the silence.

In my diaries I recorded my experiences in poetry and art – a totally inadequate exposition for something that cannot be fully expressed in either.

I persist with this inadequacy, through words, to convey some semblance of the experience.

Before I took my leave from the ashram the *Swami* asked to speak to me. He described my experiences in complete, precise detail and arranged a parting ceremony - an initiation to receive the grace of a guru through the name assigned to me: *Prem Chaitania*. My wisdom friends were delighted by this.

My teachers informed me that the *Gayatri* would continue to work on my consciousness, whether I was aware of it or not.

Any awareness would provide an arrow of insight into further changes.

There were other perceptual and cognitive experiences that I am not at liberty to communicate, and still others that I choose not to relate.

Training with *Gayatri* had major life changing effects, not the least being that I became a better and more skillful teacher, both to meditation and university students.

What I can say from personal experience is that once my wild mind was reined in, clarity and compassion were suddenly there in greater compass.

This provided a different basis for how to be with the planet and others in a new way.

This partial account of my journey in India is to demonstrate that my activism for peace, planetary care and social justice now came from a different place as a result of the internal work.

It also propels me to serve the planet and humanity in a way of creating bridges and pathways of harmony that make sense.

My work in progress is ongoing, anchored by my journeys.

PART THREE - HELLO DARKNESS

Extinction can impact us in many different ways. Our minds can destroy us as devastation shatters our will to continue. Then we find ourselves stepping back into hell's dreadful desolation, where we do not allow anyone to help us. We enable self-destruction when hope drains away. Yet there is always a glimpse, a possibility of stepping through the darkness and touching a warm, knowing light that spurs us on. I offer four short stories that move in this direction. Chapter Six: Love Lost and Dark Shadows catches the downhill lapse of a beloved seaman. Chapter Seven: The Solace of Winter has a pinnacle soaring that is then spurned. Chapter Eight: Torched is a sharp, flash fiction of desperation. Chapter 9: The Ewe permits the option of death to merge with surprising awakening.

Chapter Six: Love Lost and Dark Shadows

They left the dance and walked the hill to sit and look at the moon over the sea.

Andrew's jacket was about her shoulders as the sea and land exchanged their silences. He kissed her gently and his lips burned at the touch of her.

There was a tumult in his chest as her beauty and independence drew him to her and the demands of their waking hearts and strong young limbs could not be denied. They made love to one another, sweetly and tenderly. The heather pillowed their beauty as they reached up to the universe of stars that drew a dreamlike blanket over them.

Andrew looked at the delicate and beautiful face cradled in his arms and picked a buttercup and placed it on her lips, and kissed the flower. He kissed her cheek and teased her gently.

"Will you be my flower now Catriona?"

"You must say that to every girl you take to the heather," she retorted.

There was more than teasing in her reply. There was wistfulness. Her heart welled with love for him, for his gentleness and tenderness but she sensed he had this for everyone and wanted to be more to him than just everyone. He chuckled at her reply for he knew it was wrong though it was believed of him.

They lay side by side in the heather on that warm summer's night cradled by the moon's glow. Andrew talked of the stars and the sea and of how one day he would write of the things he felt and opened himself to Catriona. She had never seen this depth in him before and was a little afraid that she could not follow him.

But his voice softly caressed her and she regained her strength and love as she listened to him. They were with one another often after that. His mother, Annie, was pleased as she scented marriage between them, but Andrew had no thoughts for settling down. He simply delighted in being with Catriona, yet the small spark that she had lit in him grew faster than his mind allowed.

Two months later she was not there to meet his fishing boat when he docked at the pier. He was surprised by this and could not wait to see her, yet had to remain aboard until every task had been completed. Such was his way. He quickly strode to her house and was told she had taken a walk to the hills. He followed the directions given and he trod the path that led him to where they had first loved. He found her sitting there looking out to sea. She was very quiet and composed, pale and ill. He saw this and approached her quickly and sat beside her. "What is it Catriona that makes you so forlorn?" She did not answer him so that he had to move in front of her to face her. There was such concern and tenderness in his voice. He saw the tears in her eyes and softly insisted she tell him.

"I'm having a baby Andrew. I'm two months pregnant by you," they had only made love that one time, here in this place.

"Is that why you came here?" he asked.

She nodded through her tears. He reached out to her and touched her cheek with his fingers so that she would look at him. When she did he smiled.

"We'll be wed Catriona and I'll be lucky to have you as a wife." She moved away from his touch.

"Just like that? We'll be wed. Not I love you Catriona. Not will you marry me. Just we'll be wed because you've bairned me. You'd wed any girl on this island that you bairned. I'm no different am I?"

Her heart was breaking as she spoke these words to him. He was taken aback and stumbled clumsily over words, but she would rebuff him so.

"Please listen Catriona, my words are clumsy but can you not see what's in my heart? I want you for my own. I want you as my wife. I've not known how to ask you."

Catriona pulled her cardigan tightly around her body.

"Don't tell me that, for it's not so. You don't understand yourself. You love everyone. You would marry fat Jessie with the warts and be content. I-I must have more than that for I love you completely, whereas you cannot love me more than anyone else. It's not kindness I want, it's your love - all of it. I'll not be like other women and accept less or tie a man with bairns and be happy with a small piece of his affection. I want more than men are prepared to give."

Andrew implored her to believe him that she had lit a spark that coursed and burned through all of him. But Catriona believed him not. So he left her to herself and she waited for him. For two days she waited for him in quiet desperation and panic, and when he did not come she took herself to Glasgow.

She was gone several weeks, a time that Andrew passed in utmost misery. This was all beyond his understanding. She returned pale and brittle and he went to her and they walked to their place in the heather for they knew not how to talk. Andrew could not stand it. With a cry he held her and begged her to give him her love, he could not bear her so distant from him. Her hands trembled as she touched him. His heart drained at the sadness in her large blue eyes as he stood before her.

"I've had an abortion Andrew."

Time stopped. The rocks and earth absorbed her words. He stood stupidly looking at her, not seeing or hearing but frozen and rooted like a dead tree.

"An abortion. In Glasgow," she whispered.

His hand, driven by his seaman's strength, moved through the air and he hit her and felled her. He recoiled and then looked in horror at the hand that had struck his Catriona.

"Oh God forgive me. Jesus save me," he cried as he moved to pick her up. "Forgive me Catriona, please forgive me. My hand had a mind of its own. Oh, Catriona wait for me."

There was blood on her lips and teeth as she backed away from him. She was like a wounded tigress and she had no mercy or forgiveness.

"Catriona for God's sake what is happening? I want to be your husband and enjoy our bairns. What in Jesus's name have you done. Why have you done this to me?"

"To you!" she cried. She stepped towards him. The bruise from his hand had reddened her face from chin to eyebrow.

"To you! Nothing has been done to you. I did it to me, Andrew, not to you and I'll carry the sin of it to my grave."

Andrew stumbled back at her fierceness.

"I did it to me, do you hear!" she shouted and the wind took her words and the sea received them. "I did it to me!" They faced one another with dangerous intensity.

"Why Catriona, tell me why?" There were tears running down his face.

"You ask why. It's so I'm free of marrying you, so that you are free of marrying me because I'm with child. We're not for one another and the child would have bound us."

Andrew fell to his knees on the ground before her. His tears turned to a strangled sob and he cried as though his very guts would come through his mouth. He cried in this terrible fashion and collapsed prostrate on the ground with his face in the soft earth. His hands reached out and he held her foot with one hand and ground the hand that hit her into the earth. She flinched at his touch but watched his demented torment as he wept. It was just as her own when she had stumbled away from the abortionist's house, a tired Glasgow doctor who at least spared her from the horrors of the back streets.

Andrew wept as something precious and rare was lost from him and Catriona and he did not know why. They sat together - terrible in their shared pain. Soon Andrew was silent. He rested his head on her legs. He was stunned but could think of nothing but Catriona and the child they could have had. He spoke to her through great pain. He tried to lift her burden to his own shoulders so that she may have peace. He felt her desperation and pain and asked her to accept him, pledging his life and strength to her if she would take him. He stood and placed his arm protectively around her and he stroked her hair while he begged forgiveness and sought her love. She shook her head slowly, her eyes full of sadness and pain.

"There can be no going back, Andrew. This will always lie between us."

He protested that this was not so, that they needed the other to heal and grow but already his hold on Catriona was loosening.

Her heart already broken she whispered "It's no use," with a finality that he should have fought. He should have torn the barriers down, but never, ever should he have accepted her desperate words as final. As proud young persons they did not even seek help from those close to them – his mother Annie with her intuition and her uncle Colin with his worldly wisdom. And so they forgot their beauty and hurled themselves into a hell that scarred them deeply for life.

There were times his soul talked to him, to go to her wherever she was. She had been hurt as he had been hurt and she needed him as he needed her. But so convinced was he of her hate that he let her go and he bore within himself the guilt of what he had done. It was to free him she said, so his was the pain and the guilt and the deep, enduring sorrow. And for the second time he did not go to her and she disappeared from the island, but never from his mind and heart. His loss became a memory that turned into a scar that would not heal.

He returned to the sea. The dark shadow of self-contempt seeped into his relations with other men. On board the boats he drove the crew to the very limits of their endurance and they learned to fear rather than love him. He had no regard for his own safety and little for theirs, yet they remained with him, to protect him. They sensed something terrible had happened, which he would not speak of. The harder he became the more successfully did he sweep the sea of its bounty and men followed him now more for wealth and not for respect.

There were whispers that he would go the way of his father's madness, so grim and distant did he become. He bled for Catriona and when no-one saw he cried for her, for he did not understand what he could have done. He never forgave himself for striking her with his hand.

His mother Annie gave him comfort as she had as a child. She did not understand his pain at losing Catriona but for once left her tongue still. She looked after him, providing glimpses to step through the darkness around him.

Had she known the cause she would have taken him to Catriona herself. She would have understood as only a woman could the need and love that the girl's bitterness shielded. But Annie never knew and stilled her tongue when it should have probed and demanded knowledge.

Andrew lived thus, only half a man, crushing the sensitivity and poetry in his soul and driving all but his mother away from him. He could not let them see into the dark window of his soul. Thus he suffered. His mother worried at his state yet knew he was on a path that few men could step, so let his suffering be. As the years passed Annie became frail and sombre but her son saw nothing of this, so enmeshed was he in his self-disgust.

She would walk to the point by the bay to look for his boat passing through the sound even when she knew he was not to be expected. She walked in memory of her late husband Angus, who had died suddenly after coming down with catatonic mental illness. She called to mind where they had kissed when young and longed to be united with him again.

Only her frail flesh prevented her final journey and oft times she was impatient that she should still live. Just as quickly she would brush away her blasphemy and thank her God for life.

Ten years later she mused once again on these thoughts, as she rested at the point, looking to the sea. She was startled to see Andrew's boat approaching the sound and she hastily rose to return home to prepare a dinner for him.

As she turned to hurry along the path, a swift immense stroke came over her and she slowly crumpled to the ground. She regained consciousness and struggled to her feet, cursing her fainting, barely noticing that her left arm and leg moved only with great difficulty.

She sensed her late husband close by and thought little of her painful progression along the path. As she opened the garden gate a final, massive stroke hit her overburdened heart. The sky revolved about her and with relief she sank to the earth and met her Angus.

Andrew's boat had passed through the sound and made for the fishing grounds to the south west. He was there for two days and returned to dock on the third day. He left his crew to take the catch to market and walked home. He noticed the hens clamouring in the large shed and saw they had no feed, and he wondered where his mother was. He stopped to fill their bowls and drinking trays.

In the byre the cow moaned softly in subdued pain and he went to her. Her udders were swollen with unreleased milk and he took the stool and milked her until she was at last without hurt. He entered the house and called to his mother. There was no answer. He crossed to the back door and stepped into the garden.

Then he saw her huddled by the gate. Though rigor mortis had set in, Annie was leaning against the gate with a faint smile on her face. Andrew picked her up and blindly carried her into the house, setting her gently upon her bed. He tried to straighten her limbs but could not. He had no heart to cry or weep or think. He stood in her bedroom with his head bowed and the breath came thickly and heavily from his chest.

"Why?"

The small thought was released to his mind and built up in his head, growing larger and louder until it exploded from his lips.

"Why?"

His hands gripped the back of the chair he was leaning on as he bellowed in rage, voice to his wrath, pain and sorrow.

"Why?"

He picked up the chair and hurled it through the window. The shattering of the glass drew him to more destruction. The only act of being he possessed was to destroy and he bellowed and roared through the house, smashing and breaking with his great strength. His mother lay dead and at peace while he destroyed whatever was about him.

Old Colin, ill in bed, heard him from his own farm house and stumbled from his sickness to limp up the track to Andrew's house. He heard the bellows and roars of an animal in fury and could scarce believe it was Andrew. He entered the house and saw the devastation. Standing in the midst of it was his young friend, who had courted his niece Catriona many years past. Andrew's wild eyes caught the old man and it was almost with a triumph that he pointed to his mother's room. Colin entered and his heart filled with grief to see Annie so. He also saw the look of peace on her face, and briefly knelt to pray for her soul.

"Why, Colin?"

It was an urgent desperate whisper from Andrew. At Colin's silence the storm of wrath swept his voice to a roar.

"Is there a curse on our family?" he shouted at the old man. "What have we done to deserve this? My father mad, now this my mother."

Colin started to speak, to calm him, but the anger and grief were too strong.

"Everyone I touch suffers, even your niece Catriona."

Colin looked sharply at him. It was a decade since Catriona left the island. Andrew could not go on, finished at the mention of Catriona's name. Colin led him away and called for others to see to Annie and to the destruction in the house. He tried to reach the young man he loved but there were barriers, grief and torment that he could not cross. Andrew stumbled away from him, from his house and drowned himself in the oblivion that drink is kind enough to give. In whisky and gin and finally in anything that had a taste of alcohol, he found a place to keep himself away from pain.

He drank while he was awake and slept wherever he fell - in ditches, on doorsteps, on kitchen floors. His kinsfolk and friends tried to reach him, to bring him back. Oh, how they tried. But he had locked himself from them and answered their kindness with abuse and drunkenness. His boat lay at the dock for fully a month until the mate went out with her. Still his folk gave only kindness, and it was kindness that eventually let him be, to wander and shuffle about the island from croft to pub, pub to dock, pier to pub, in a constant never ending oblivion of drink and delirium.

The islanders bore his pain with him, caring for him, but he would not let their love come to him. He had failed them. The animals at his farm were the only creatures that kept him this side of sanity as he tended to their needs. In rare moments of sobriety he fished for himself, setting lines and traps for lobsters, crabs and cod in the sea near his house. It was pathetic that he, the best fisherman in the islands, should cast a line from a small dinghy. But he did it and took some solace in his return to a primitive survival. He set the lines further out to sea and rowed his dinghy to lift the sea's gift.

His judgment and seamanship had become careless, almost as if he willingly dropped his guard for the sea to deliver the blow he longed for. He took no notice of the bank of dark streaked clouds that reared suddenly in the sky. He took his oars and rowed out to sea. The clouds darkened as a rapidly advancing front of cold air lifted the warm front that hung over the sea. It tossed violently to the sky and created sudden and vicious turbulence. Still Andrew did not notice, not until he felt the dinghy being moved and driven by power not from his arms. The quick winds had caught the tail of the ebb tide and they ran in opposed directions with the small dinghy caught between them. The swell of the sea that had been hardly visible before now rose in ugly and menacing ridges of water that raced straight for the boat. Andrew turned the prow of the boat into the huge swell. As he fought to keep the boat into the swell one of his oars snapped in two. He slowly straightened with the broken oar in his hand and he saw in the sea his chance to end it all.

"Take me," he bellowed. "Finish it and give me peace."

The boat turned sluggishly and was hit beam on by the next wave and spun into the trough, keeling dangerously to one side but it righted itself and rolled over the top of the swell. He was now standing, waiting.

The boat turned too slowly for the next wave that towered above it. Andrew welcomed it as a huge hammer blow split the boat's keel from its beam. As the boat rose in the air with its back broken, he was hurled into the sea. Gratefully he went down and did not struggle against the cold grip the sea had on him. He came to the surface and felt nothing. He wondered if he was already dead. The current that ran there swept him towards some tidal reefs, battering his body on the outcrops of rock and leaving him atop a slime-covered skerrie.

The sea continued to crash over him, but with less intensity as the tide fell. He was alive. The sea would not take him. He waited for the tide to turn again and before it could advance he had clambered over the skerries and swam to the shore. He dragged himself painfully to his house, delirious and incoherent and would let no man help him until he had drunk himself into a stupor.

Once drunk, he knew they could not help him. He continued his course of self-destruction for many years until finally folk learned to ignore him, and forgot what he once was and could have been.

Yet he saw himself one night in the bar of the pub, and was astonished at what he saw. His mind floated free from his body and rested to look at himself. He saw a terrible, ragged, pathetic creature stumbling from table to table slobbering stupidly, begging for a drink. His mind took this in but slowly. That's not me. It cannot be me. The mind gasped.

Is this the first that you have seen of yourself these past years? Look well Andrew. Look well on what you have destroyed in becoming as you are.

He saw himself fall over a table and bring the glasses of beer and whisky spilling into the laps of the men drinking there. With a curse an Aberdeen fisherman with beer splashed over him took Andrew by the shoulders and shook him and ordered him away.

Andrew saw his body and face standing there, stupidly grinning at the east coast man still begging for a drink. He did not feel the punch that split his nose and sent him crashing into another table. He rolled over and got to its feet, still grinning stupidly as the blood ran from its face.

Eight strong island men moved towards his tormentor and threw the man from Aberdeen and his friends from that place. They were ashamed of Andrew but he was their own and in their pity and disgust they protected him and took the wreck of a man home, leaving him at the door of his house.

With sadness and loathing they walked away. Andrew slobbered and grinned stiffly through caked blood and alcohol.

We took him into his house and left him there for the different parts of his soul to do battle with the other. There was nothing that man and conscience could do. So we left him there, seeing himself anew. In the very depths of hell we left him there.

Chapter Seven: The Solace of Winter

The wind from the north soughed softly along the shore but froze any man it gripped.

Snow lay in drifts, piled deep to the spine of Mount Doracher. A mire of ice covered the window panes. The cold stole into every door and numbed the hands and minds of those unprepared for it. No winter had been like this.

Donald stood by his window and breathed on the window pane to melt the frost. He saw a fringe of ice skirting the bay below his house. There was a stoop to his shoulders and his clothes were unkempt.

He lifted his coat and scarf from a chair and put them on. He pushed his bed away from the fire that was now cold. The room was untidy and dirty with newspapers and dishes strewn about the place.

Breathing heavily from the cold he lit the fire, humming tonelessly to himself, indifferent to the squalor around him. In this, his sixty-eighth year, he simply did not care. No one came there anymore and he chose not to go anywhere. His face was heavily lined, older than its years.

His mouth pursed as he sucked at his teeth waiting for the fire to catch. He grunted in pleasure as the flames grew. He spread his large, weathered hands before him to catch their warmth.

Then, he shuffled into the kitchen and coaxed a paraffin burner to life and placed a kettle of water on it to boil. He waited, not even thinking of the day and what he had to do. His responses to the seasons and their demands were automatic and often without thought.

Donald waited in his freezing kitchen for the boiling kettle, then took his cup and made tea. He collected a large spoon and took a pot of cold stew from the pantry and shuffled back to the fire. He sat on his bed and breakfasted on the cold, greasy lamb stew and left the pot by the fire.

He drank slowly from his large cup then prepared for the cold. He lined his boots and socks with newspapers and put a layer between his shirt and jacket, and stepped outside. He gasped as the cold hit him and he made hurriedly to the byre. The animals there shuddered at the raw blast as the door opened but quickly recognized him. His hens boldly gathered about him. He talked to them, reaching to the loft for their feed and water.

He set their feed before them and searched their nesting places in the crannies of the byre for their eggs. They offered large brown eggs to this man with the soft voice and gentle hands. He collected a basketful of eggs before taking hay into his cow. He put the hay in her manger and ran his hand over her back and flanks. She lowed softly and turned to rub her head on his leg before picking at the hay. He cleaned the manure from her stall and put fresh water in the trough. The byre was cleaner than his house and some nights he would sleep there next to the sound and warm smell of his animals. He milked the cow, pressing his face to her flank while his strong fingers drew milk from her swollen udders. He hummed a tune that once he danced to, drawing life and vigour from the company of beasts. He left the cow munching at her hay and placed the two buckets, one with eggs, the other overflowing with milk, on a shelf by the door. Taking a half filled sack of cob nuts he braced himself again for the cold.

He trudged away from the byre, feeling the cold's bite. He searched for the dozen sheep he still kept, thinking of where they would be sheltering from the snow and cold.

Then, he climbed the ridge that separated his house from the rest of the village, noticing clumps of moss underfoot and icicles hanging from fences. He looked down on desolation. No smoke rose from any chimney. Nobody lived there any longer. They had left or died. Fences hung in disrepair and empty houses gave themselves to the ravages of time. He shielded his eyes from the snow's glare and looked for his sheep. In the distance some four miles away he could make out the thin ribbon of the new road, built to take tourists more rapidly from one end of the island to the other, cutting off his village. But it mattered not. Donald was the only one left in the village. He shunned the company of men, preferring his solitude and isolation. He was warmed only by nature and his animals and had long ceased to think about the world he had turned his back on.

Donald saw his sheep huddled for warmth in the lee of a deserted croft house and he picked his way through the snow drifts towards them. The wind had dropped and the sweat from his body had turned his layers of newspaper to a spongy mass. He shivered as he threw them away. The sheep had seen him and galloped towards him, some floundering in drifts in their eagerness to reach him. He patiently dug them out and fed them by hand from the sack he carried. He led them to a deserted house and opened the door so that they could shelter there. He counted them. They were all there. He shivered as he sat there pressed against them for warmth. His sack was empty but still his creatures ferreted for more. He laughingly pushed them away and stood up to go. He noticed a change in the sky that heralded more snow and pulled his coat about him a little tighter.

He wondered if the post van would have left his supplies by the road. It came with groceries once a week and the driver would leave a box of bare essentials for the man he rarely saw, taking his dues from the weekly cheque from the district office that he cashed for Donald. The two men would hardly talk on the rare occasions they met but there was a subliminal trust between them. If Donald did not have money then he would leave a basket of eggs, a shoulder of mutton or a box of filleted fish and the van driver would arrive at an adequate recompense. This primitive form of barter suited both parties. He walked the few remaining miles to the road leaving the sheep in the deserted house. Broken fence frames stuck out from the grip of the snow, wooden sheep pens, broken and derelict, groaned with the ice expanding in their seams. Donald had long ago accepted this neglect and desolation.

He arrived at the road and saw that a cardboard box had been left for him. He opened it and examined every article before putting them in his sack. There was flour, butter, sugar, tea, nails, cartridges and a large jar of home-made jam. He smiled at this and muttered to himself, "Nice man that driver. I must leave a lobster for him one of these days."

Donald transferred the sack to his back and walked hurriedly to his croft. Already the day's light was disappearing. It began to snow as he walked half frozen the five miles to where he remained the sole human survivor. His hands and feet were numb and his eyes staring as he gulped great breaths of air into his lungs on his steady trudge home. He reached his door and fumbled with useless fingers at the latch until it yielded to admit him.

His fire was all but out though he had banked it with slow-burning peats. It had taken him longer to struggle to the road and back than he had anticipated. He took paper and thrust it under a still smouldering peat. His hands could not grip his box of matches and while he tried again and again to take a match between his fingers the paper took flame from the peat. Gratefully he bent to it, placing small sticks round the flame, building it up to take peats that were stacked by the fire. The warmth shot through his hands like a pain as the cold thawed from him. He shuddered at the sensations in his body but did not move away until the flames cast their warmth to the room. He hung the pot of cold stew on a hook above the fire and added flour and salt to his greasy mixture.

While it cooked he went outside again, to the byre, to feed his animals and bring back the eggs and milk. He was tired. The cold had drained and sapped him. It was with relief that he finally closed his door for the night, stuffing paper and rags into the gaps through which winter's fingers would poke. An involuntary shiver passed through him as he sat on his bed before the fire.

His stew boiled and he ate ravenously, spooning it straight from the pot to his mouth, soaking lumps of bread into the gravy and eating them with his fingers. He carried the empty pot to the kitchen and took a long drink from the bucket of milk. It left a white stain around his lips which he wiped with his sleeve. He belched in satisfaction and wearily returned to the warmth. As the fire continued to burn he lay fully clothed on the bed and pulled the heavy blankets over him. He slept the dreamless sleep of the weary.

The winter seemed to never end. Donald was desperate for the spring to come. He needed the signs of continuity and life to guide him on his own peculiar struggle for survival. He had forgotten why he had become so separate from friends and family, if indeed any decision had consciously been made. He had clung to his father's barren farm, to the hills and his animals and they had nurtured him in a way that human company could not. He was not unhappy, neither was he happy – he was simply content to survive.

"Letter for you."

Donald was standing by the road basking in the first signs of spring as the van driver pulled up. The driver climbed out of the van with a sack of provisions under one arm and a letter clutched in his other hand. The deep cold of winter had thawed, allowing the first daffodils to poke their heads above ground with their dormant yellow splendour. The thaw had not penetrated Donald. He stood uneasily in the spring sunshine, staring at the letter held out to him. He slowly took the envelope and a faint uneasy memory stirred in him as he recognized the writing.

"I believe it's from your sister," said the van driver.

Donald nodded in agreement and stood still for a moment as he wondered why she would write to him. He stuffed it into his pocket and collected his sack of provisions, then without a word walked away from the van. The driver shook his head slowly at Donald's retreating back and got out to collect the bucket of eggs left there for him. Behind the bucket was a large lobster. Its claws were bound and the antennae on its head moved slowly when he picked it up. The driver again shook his head at the strangeness of the man he would have liked to know better.

There was turmoil in Donald's mind as he walked to his desolate home. *Moira, his sister, had written him. It had been thirty years or more since he had seen her.* The letter remained unread for several days, sitting underneath a cup on the mantelpiece with other letters he had received through the years and had never opened.

He went about his daily round with his animals and his lobster traps, taking care of the creatures that sustained him. He caught the changing tide in a small rowing boat he had salvaged. He carefully placed several traps by a rock skerrie where he knew the first lobsters of spring would be hiding.

But the letter from Moira kept drifting into his mind. It lay neglected on the mantle until he could stand it no longer and hurried home from the oar he was mending and he took the letter down. He opened it and read what Moira had to say, admiring the roundness of her script. She had been to the island several times but could never bring herself to cross the gulf that now separated them. She had seen him from the road last summer.

"So that was the well-dressed lady, who stared at me so long," mused Donald.

She wanted to see him. She was widowed. She would come in the late Autumn. She did not expect that he would meet her at the ferry.

"No I wouldn't do that, right enough," he muttered to himself. She would make her own way.

He read the letter several times before placing it back underneath the cup. He rubbed his hand over the stubble on his chin.

"I must shave for when she comes, aye, and clean this place up."

He glanced round at the midden he inhabited and smiled ruefully to himself. He liked his walls and took comfort from the simple homeliness of the clutter.

Donald talked and chuckled to himself as he imposed a certain tidiness and cleanliness to his home. All for his sister's visit, late in Autumn.

He was harvesting his main crop of potatoes when he saw her walk from a car that stopped at the road. He went to meet her and greeted her shyly, unsure of what to say to his sister. He admired the cut of her expensive suit and sensible walking shoes and guided her along the path to the house where they had both been children. They talked easily about their lives and different fortunes, letting the other only glimpse the surface and not the depths.

Donald had not talked for such length for many years and was mildly exhilarated at using vocabulary long neglected. He noted that time had not been kind to Moira. Her face was drawn and he saw bitterness in her gaunt eyes that did not reflect the dignity and grace of her expensive clothes.

He led her through the door of the house. There was a large bucket of marsh flowers by the fireplace. He had picked them that morning from the marsh, remembering her love for them. He had re-arranged the house so that its comfort would welcome a visitor. Moira looked around and wrinkled her nose in distaste.

"The same old sticks and ugly furniture. How can you live with it Donald?"

His heart sank with disappointment.

"It suits me well enough for what I want."

"That is quite evident." She answered waspishly. Her own house in a fashionable area of Glasgow was polished and gleaming, expensive and cold. Correct for mid-day bridge with her ladies' committees. A burnished reflection of the constant show to paper over the void of life that she had never lived. Her escape from the poverty of her island life had not provided freedom from her bitterness.

She couldn't help but to walk round the room and into the kitchen, inspecting the carpets, chairs and ragged curtains.

"You should get rid of all this. I'll send you what you need from Glasgow. Don't worry, I'll pay. The least I can do for my neglect of you."

Donald was stunned and stood in helpless silence at his sister's verbal destruction of things that satisfied him.

He said gently,

"Is that all you can see, Moira? These sticks you despise are just simple parts of what I have here. I'm content with them. If they offend you, look not at them. Did you see the irises in the bucket there? I picked them for you this morning. You used to like them."

She turned and looked at his gesture and felt the mildness of his soft rebuke. She bit her lips and tried to control the mounting venom that came to her tongue. How dare he live in this simplicity? Who was he to turn his back on the world and live just as he pleased?

"Why do you stay here, cut off from everything?" She blurted out.

He shrugged and took his time to answer.

"I don't really know why, it just seemed to happen that way." He answered simply. His mildness and gentleness were a spur to Moira's deep well of bitterness.

"I'll tell you why," she snapped.

"You're hiding here in this hovel. You could never leave this island because deep down you're a total failure."

She paused for breath unable to stop the bitterness she felt.

"Out there is a world that takes guts and backbone. You-you're spineless." She stopped for a moment at the look of amazement on her brother's face. "You could have been the best fisherman in the Minch. But look at you. Secluded here with your sheep subsidies and quiet. You would be exposed anywhere else for what you are. A failure. That's what keeps you and everybody else here on this island."

She finished with a sharp edge to her words, intended to cut her brother.

Slowly Donald understood the well of bitterness that his sister drew from. With quiet composure he spoke.

"If that is so, then why is it necessary for you come back to reveal this truth to me, Moira? Why do you think you have to make sure I understand why I am here?" At her silence he continued. "I'll tell you why. There's a simplicity here that offends you, that reminds you of where you came from, an honesty before God that you fear to recognize. This is a rebuke to the empty round of shallow posters you fill your life with. That's why you come back to this island. To fill your emptiness, to scoff at simplicity, while you snatch at it for yourself."

The colour mounted on Moira's cheeks as his voice grew more insistent.

"There's a reminder here, of what you once were and could have been and that's too much for a creature like you to accept. You chose your life, ashamed of us here but you know full well where the balance of truth lies."

There was a hushed silence filled only with their emotions and strain.

They were both right. They faced one another across the kitchen table, the same one they had cracked crab claws on when they were children. The fury and shock of their words made them tremble. Moira's lips quivered as she choked off a retort and hurriedly she turned away from Donald's piercing eyes and words.

He let out a long breath and stepped to Moira's side and put his hand on her arm.

"What are we saying to one another Moira? Thirty years and all we do is hurt? We've learned very little then. Come and walk to the shore with me and let the autumn breeze take the evil from our tongues."

Moira nodded through her trembling and reluctantly followed her brother. They walked slowly and Moira slipped her hand through his arm. He pointed out things to her - gently reminding her of what she had come from. Easing her mind with stories of the sheep running away with the washing and rabbiting with their brother Angus. They stood by the shore. Two figures in middle age briefly united in a semblance of peace.

"Well Moira, I may be a bit of a failure in some eyes."

"No, no Donald please let me take back my words I didn't mean to..."

"You can have back the pain, my sister, but not the words. There's some truth in them. But realize that here in a terrible fashion to you and others I at least survive in the shadow of truth and eternity. Derelict and simpleton that I appear, I might just understand a little of the way of things."

They stood in silence for a long time, tired and spent from their emotions. He walked with her to the road where her car was parked. They were at last strangely comfortable with one another.

"I've a favour to ask of you."

He stopped and listened.

"My youngest son is with me on the island."

There was a note of distaste in her voice that puzzled him.

"He's a businessman and has bought the schoolhouse at the head of the next bay to you. He wants to set up a shellfish factory and needs a site and a deep water landing stage for fishing boats. It would bring business and employment to the island." She finished feebly.

Donald looked at her sharply. The only location for such an access was on his farm, the north side of the bay below his house. There the rock plunged vertically into the sea, a natural anchorage for fishing vessels, a haven yet for cormorants and guillemots.

"No," she added, "that's not why I came to see you. I came to see you for myself, but will you meet with him?"

Donald nodded and she quickly got into her car, relieved that she had accomplished her purpose. She drove away from everything she feared to be reminded of.

The smells and sounds of morning pleased Donald as he sat in the sun by his house the next day. He was cleaning his shotgun. He cocked his head to listen to the different songs of birds long awake, resting the gun across his knees. He saw lapwings soaring almost vertically to catch flying insects and high above a majestic eagle circled slowly in a sky so clear and blue.

Donald drew breath at the scent of marsh and pasture that drifted towards him. He never ceased to wonder at the regeneration the seasons were capable of. He smiled to himself as he continued to clean his gun, thinking of the mountain hares he must outwit that day.

A man, about thirty years of age, approached the house. Donald had seen him for the last mile of his long walk from the new road. As the man came nearer Donald noticed the smart blue city suit and the small green yachting boots that kept the trouser cuffs from the grass and mud.

The man was sweating heavily in the morning sun, his collar tight about his throat. He was heavily set and his breath wheezed harshly as he came to a halt in front of him. Donald inspected him more closely, noting the sleeked back hair, the carefully clipped moustache, and the shrewd, sharp eyes that lurked behind hooded lids.

"I'm your sister's son, John Menzie is my name."

The voice was soft, melodious and manipulative. It took Donald by surprise. No, this could not be Moira's son.

"Well, I'm her stepson, Moira never had children of her own."

So that's it, I was right not to recognize him as spawned from Moira. Donald pondered in silence at the soft and charming voice that he was not in the least taken in by. He shook John Menzie's hand and exchanged easy pleasantries about the weather and crops and his sister Moira. He recoiled a little at the smoothness of the man, but nothing showed in his soft blue eyes or mild expression. He listened as his sister's stepson carefully led up to his business.

It was explained to him why the access through his croft was so important to John Menzie's business venture.

Donald allowed the music of the man's voice to continue without his full attention. He patiently listened to the economics of shell fishing, the employment it would bring and the new life and prosperity it would promise. Menzie had already established small ventures on the island that tied in with his mainland business.

"Will it be your money that will pay for all this?" Donald asked.

A quick frown wrinkled Menzie's forehead and he replied:

"Not exactly, there's government grants and employment grants for starting something new in an area like this. It just needs someone like me to start it. With present prices for shellfish, a factory here couldn't fail. There'll be quite a bit of my own money as well, but most of it will be from the government."

Menzie grinned in an assumed compliance, and added:

"It's time something was put back into these islands. Well, shall we walk over to where the site would be and I'll show you what I have in mind?"

118

Donald reluctantly complied. Menzies seemed not to notice his reticence as he talked of bookkeeping procedures that would bring in the most profit, the money in it for Donald and the good it would do for the island community.

At the other side of the bay John Menzie paced out the factory's location, how simple and quick then to transfer the fish from a jetty that would be next to the natural landing stage. He was thorough and persuasive and Donald admired his skill. But it was only with half an ear that he listened. He heard the wash of the sea on the rocks and looked at the welter of flowers about him, whose regimes changed with every summer month. He was no longer attentive to the words of the young man. His mind was open to a different reality. They walked back from the bay. Menzie felt pleased, mistaking reticence for acceptance.

"You'll think it over? There'll be quite a pocket full of money for you if this goes through."

"Oh, I don't think that's at all necessary."

"This is business, you know," Menzie smiled expansively.

"You do not understand me Mr. Menzie, I do not wish my pockets to be full. There will not be any jetty on my land for your factory."

They were back by the house. John Menzie stood in silence, but only for a moment.

"Why not?"

There was no melody in the voice now, just a controlled harshness. Donald took his time, picking up his shotgun to resume its cleaning.

"There may be a lot you think I don't understand but this much I do know. You will no doubt be here to receive the government's bounty in the name of helping this island. But I will not expect you to be here the moment there is a draw on your own finances."

He looked shrewdly at the young man whose face was reddening with anger.

> "Dreams will be raised, there'll be a brief life for a few families but you will leave richer and it will be this island that will remain poor. It is better that the flowers and gulls maintain their ascendancy on that bit of my land. They have more respect for it than you."

A mixture of emotion struggled for expression in John Menzie's face. He burst out angrily,

> "You bloody old fool. Do you think you can hold back progress?"

Donald smiled at him and said slowly.

> "I think I may be just doing that very thing."

> "You'll not stop me, there are other places and other people who can use money," Menzie snarled.

Donald calmly indicated with the gun barrel that the conversation was over. Menzie stood for only a moment before striding swiftly away, his green yachting boots brought a smile of amusement from Donald as he lifted the gun. A blast from the shotgun roared over the morning's stillness.

Menzie threw himself to the ground and rolled into a ditch, and frantically searched himself for pellet wounds. There were none. Slowly he drew himself erect and looked back to where the old man stood with the shotgun in his hands. Donald pointed to the hare that lay twitching in its death throes not thirty yards from the ditch that harboured Menzie.

> "It's a terrible mess you're making of your fine suit, Mr. Menzie," he called.

Menzie noticed the green slime on his shoulder and mud on his knees and in fury strode to the already dead hare and was due to kick it until he noticed the shotgun aimed casually in his direction. He spun on his heel and quickened his step. Every time he turned to look over his shoulder he would see the old man stalking him, keeping an easy pace with him. Twice more the shotgun roared, and twice more did John Menzie throw himself to the ground only to have yet another dead hare pointed out to him.

Menzie reached the road panting in fury and hysteria. Moira was there with the car. She had watched her stepson set the hares coursing for her brother's gun and relished that her arrogant stepson should be reduced to a frustrated sobbing mass. He climbed into the seat beside her, struggling for control.

She sat silent, coolly smoking a cigarette. She did not offer her stepson one as she waited for her brother to walk to the car. He came slowly with the shotgun in the crook of his arm and stood by her window.

"It's a fine day Moira."

"Not if you are a hare or a businessman, surely."

He chuckled softly at her humour.

"Here's something for your dinner."

"It's a good day for shooting, Donald."

"It is at that."

They enjoyed an almost private amusement, ignoring the man staring fixedly through the windscreen. Moira exulted in her brother's surprising invincibility and accepted the hares he held out to her. She smiled openly at him, her brother, without guile or bitterness tracing her features.

"Thank you Donald and God's blessings with you."

"And with you Moira."

She drove away. He knew he would not see her again but rejoiced that they could give God's blessing to one another.

Donald glanced at the darkening autumn sky and knew there would soon be a first snow on Mount Doracher.

He smiled to himself and returned to his solitude and isolation, relieved once more to shun the company of his fellow men.

Torched

She recognized the unmistakable gait of the man walking toward her on the beach.

"Callum, what are you doing?" she exclaimed.

He snapped round, trying to hide the petrol can in his hand. Sweat was breaking out on his face and in his armpits. He muttered a curse and shouted angrily,

"It's none of your fucking business. Get away from me." His handsome face was twisted with fear.

She pointed to the petrol can and asked his intentions

He trembled, all six feet of him, in fear of the determined young woman who had caught him. His jeans and work boots had splashes of petrol on them and his dark eyes flickered desperately around to see if anyone else had seen him.

"I have to set the house up there ablaze. The owner has not paid his dues to the land owner." Then with a touch of shame, "It's my job to do this. There is nothing else for me on this god-forsaken island."

"You will not torch the old man's house."

Callum breathed heavily several times before replying,

"If I do not, you know that it will be me that gets torched. That's how it works."

The silence was vibrant with anger, fear and shame. At last she spoke:

"How far you have fallen Callum – you need help."

He stepped towards her, desperate to remember better times.

"How can you help me then?"

She took the petrol can from his hand and said,

"The old man has moved to an institution on the mainland and will not return."

He gasped with his mouth wide open when he saw her unscrew the can and splash the petrol over the wooden door and windows of the small house close to the beach. She struck a match and threw it on the petrol soaked door. The blaze lit up the sombre evening.

She walked towards the beach and passed the empty petrol can to her eldest brother.

Chapter Nine: Ewe

Catherine asked very formally if old John would care to take her for a walk. He answered,

"Of course my child," with the grave courtesy he reserved for her. They left to explore the fell, a high, largely barren landscape of moor-covered hills and patches of thickets.

She placed her small hand in old John's large and gnarled fist, eager for adventure. For his part old John loved this vivacious child who reignited something in him with her wonder at the world. They began their adventure right below the house.

Her parents, Edgar and Breanne, waved to them from the window. Breanne leaned on her husband, his arm about her waist. "You love that old man don't you Edgar." It was not a question.

"Yes. Yes I do," he replied and held her tighter.

"I'm glad. I love him too. It is beautiful to see two men unafraid of the depths of their feelings. It's a rare strength to share a legacy of experience between generations. He has so much to offer."

Edgar was silent, his wife in his arms, grateful for her understanding, not knowing how true her words would ring to change all of their lives.

Catherine and John walked further into the fell, then sat on a large boulder as they surveyed the two miles they had just come. He had explored with her eyes every hiding place and sitting place that she favoured on her walk to and from school.

Her vivaciousness delighted him as she greeted trees and rocks as old friends, markers on her wayward path to home. She pointed out trails that had a similar character to some of the island walks she had taken with John at his home in the Outer Hebrides.

Catherine loved the similar trails from both locations, as it often felt to her as though he was always right there with her. John was very moved by her accounts. He also felt the scars in his mind begin to melt away, placed there fifty years ago by losing his first love also named Catherine. He was so grateful for this child. She had brought him back to his "song" ever since she and her parents had taken refuge in his croft in the Hebrides during a severe summer storm.

John had never felt so happy since they entered his life. They had all walked together, told stories and were silent when it rained and he opened the wonders of the island to them. He and the child spent hours and days in one another's company, crossing the hills to the Atlantic Ocean rolling all the way from Newfoundland. He - slowing down and carrying her when she tired, she - with the excitement and happiness of the sun warming her.

All too soon it was over. Edgar, Breanne and Catherine left for their home in Cumberland where Edgar worked at his writing and Breanne taught music. It had been an awakening for John. In the months after they left he recalled every incident of his knowing of them. It had been so total and complete that there could be no holding back. He thought of them as he retraced the walks they took in concert, remembering the awe of the child at seeing eagles fly and gannets plunge into the sea.

He was overjoyed when they wrote to him enclosing ferry and rail tickets to come to Cumberland to be with them for the Christmas of that year. He was surprised and delighted to see Breanne on the railway platform at Glasgow and gently held her in a fond embrace.

"Did you not think I could manage these railways, eh?" he said to her in his gentle manner.

"It would be a lie to say I was here for any other purpose," she laughed gaily. They walked together along the platform and boarded the train for Carlisle where Edgar and Catherine would meet them with a car. She talked excitedly of how the island and John had filled their lives as they knew they had filled his.

Soon there was Edgar and Catherine and the simple pleasure of being with them again. They lived in a small stone cottage in the middle of Cumberland, separated from the nearest village by a long fell. Breanne taught music in the local schools, travelling from one to the other taking her gift of song and music to the eager children. She had created a small orchestra from the talent of her students, garnering gifts and donations of classical instruments so the children could play with the best. Catherine played the violin and Celtic harp and was an enthusiastic component of this small ensemble.

There was a quiet comfort in their home and community. Edgar's study with its walls lined with books had been made into a room for John. He looked round him at all the books, at the large desk facing the window that looked on to the fell. He traced his fingers over the leather bound volumes, the copies of Edgar's own work.

"I'll never leave until all these books are read."

"I wish that would be true," sighed Edgar.

John felt so at ease in this room full of books and with this man. A spark that had been doused earlier in his life was lived through the young author. Edgar took him over to his desk and showed him a manuscript for a play that was almost completed.

"John, this comes from our talking last summer. It's the best I've ever written. Look here," Edgar was excited to show how much he had been influenced by John's insights and memories. Edgar turned the page and showed the acknowledgement to their long conversations. John felt a mixture of pride and embarrassment as he read Edgar's description of him.

"It's not right Edgar," he said at last. "It's not my hand that produced this."

"Not your hand John, but your thoughts, our thoughts meeting and mingling. I simply write it down but you're as much a co-author of this as am I. It never would have occurred had I not met you."

They stood there in the warm glow of their friendship, the young man and the old man. Edgar made coffee over a burner by the side of the fireplace and handed a cup to John. Breanne and Catherine came in and joined them by the fire in the taking of coffee. The child pulled a face at the bitterness of the taste but as she was learning to be grown up she persevered.

"Did you walk down the fell John with Catherine this afternoon?" Breanne spoke to him as he sat himself comfortably in their lounge.

"We did. I liked it fine and Catherine pointed out every rock and tree that reminded her of my island. I'm thinking the fell fills with snow very quickly. I felt the menace of heavy snow in the air."

"That's what happens in bad blizzards. We can be cut off until a tractor clears a way through. Snow seems to hit the fell much more than anywhere else," Breanne explained.

A shallow dusting of snow in the air greeted them in the morning. John was surprised at the lightness of the snowfall. He felt the menace in the sky and wondered what it was being reserved for. Catherine left for school delighted at the wonder the snow gave to the branches of the trees and shapes of the rocks now that they were snow laden. She skipped away adamantly insisting that she go alone, making John promise to be there when she came back. Such a promise was easily given, as old John smiled to the child.

It was mid-morning that the threat in the sky revealed its true nature. It started to snow heavily and continued throughout the afternoon. John noted the direction of the wind. It blew directly up the path of the fell collecting every flake of heavy wet snow, piling it into drifts that the contours of the ground demanded. Catherine had a dancing class after school and they were not expecting her until evening. John worried about this. He asked Breanne what the child would do, and was only slightly relieved to hear that she would stay with friends in the village until the storm passed. The wind picked up, sucking the snow into the fell, packing it deeper and deeper into all those spots where a child would walk.

Edgar telephoned to the village. He was very quiet when he put down the phone.

"She's not there. She didn't stay for her dancing class, but left for home after her lunch." He stopped, thinking rapidly. "That's five hours ago."

They all felt a mounting alarm. Edgar and Breanne quickly dressed for the cold.

"Will you stay here John, by the phone? I'll get friends from the village to search from the bottom of the fell." At his insistence that he too would search for her, Edgar beseeched him to stay. "You're better here, John. Someone has to stay by the phone. We know the fell."

They left and searched. The wind hurled the blizzard in their eyes and they shouted out to their daughter. Edgar and Breanne stumbled into drifts, looking for signs of Catherine until they met with the searchers from the village. They were frozen and terrified for her. They beat their way slowly up the fell in a line calling to Catherine. One man went back to the village to get more help. Breanne and Edgar arrived back at their cottage and stumbled cold and numb into its grateful warmth. Nobody was there. A note was on the table. From John, it said simply:

"You may know the fell, but not through the eyes of a child."

He had watched them leave and stood by the telephone waiting for its urgent ring with news. He closed his eyes and went over in his mind the walks he had with Catherine on his island, recalling how she favoured certain paths, remembering the kind of land that drew her feet and interest. Then he went over every bit of the fell in his mind, seeing it through her eyes. He took one of Edgar's walking sticks and put on his coat, stuffing spare clothes for Catherine into a pack. Then John left for the fell.

Edgar stared at the note, then he was moved to thought and decision. There were six people there. He took a map of the fell and divided it into grids, organizing, directing. Parties of two would search each grid in relays, returning for rest and warmth to the house at hourly intervals. He picked up the phone and co-ordinated the search with police and willing helpers from the village, telling them which areas to concentrate on.

"There's my child and an old man out there. We must find them both."

John had walked directly to the edge of the fell, to the high ground. He did not look for the child but listened first of all to the direction that animals would take for shelter. He was very still within himself, allowing his keen sense of nature's rhythms to direct him.

He searched first for signs of sheep, tracing their paths to shelter, knowing Catherine would have followed them once she saw her danger. He plunged into drifts and struggled painfully out of them. He did not call or shout but strained every sense so that he could hear and feel. He found several sheep huddled together in numerous places but no Catherine.

John stood and thought deeply for a sign of the child. His eyes were drawn to a lie of the land beneath the snow that he instantly saw Catherine would take. It was the same land form that led from his croft house in the Hebrides to the bay before it. He walked steadily to it, feeling drawn by his senses and then he found her track, in concert with the steps of a sheep. He followed them both and found them together, the child and the ewe, in a shallow cave overhung with rock and turf.

She was blue with cold and huddled with the exposure to nature's indifference. He knelt beside her and felt fear at her lack of recognition of him. He blocked out the snow with his strong body and willed life to the child. He offered up a prayer of gratitude for the finding of her and crooned softly to her in his own language, singing Gaelic lullabies and island songs to her. He must not lose her. The ewe stared balefully at John and stamped her foot. He spoke softly to the creature, knowing already that he would need her if they were to live. His voice came softly through the layers of fear and cold that entrapped Catherine.

"I told you I would be waiting for you little one."

She heard his gentle voice and stirred a little. He sat beside her, noting her dullness of response, slowly warming her hands in his and gently rubbing her thin knees that were cold, so cold. Then he dressed her in the additional clothes of hers that he carried in his pack. The snow was whipped into a whirling blizzard by a wind that had no mercy. He knew they could not leave their shelter that night and they must live. His jacket and coat were wrapped round the huddled pitiful form of the child and he held her to him for warmth. The ewe was impatient to leave for fear of them but feared the blizzard more. John talked to Catherine about what they would do. They must live he told her. The ewe would give herself to them so that they could live. She must understand this. Catherine nodded while he explained to her that he was going to kill the sheep and then gut it so that she may be placed inside for warmth so that he may have his jacket and coat and not freeze. She nodded with the wisdom of a seven year old, concerned only that the sheep would not suffer.

"No, my Catherine, the ewe will not suffer."

He spoke softly to the animal and touched it gently at the ears. The ewe ceased its trembling and relaxed and while he talked to her he took his fisherman's knife and swiftly cut its jugular. While it died, his own numbed hands were restored to life by its warm blood. He gave thanks to the ewe for her life. After gutting the animal, he slit it open from the breast bone to the tail. He placed the child inside the dead carcass and she was insulated from the freezing touch of the blizzard. Mercifully she slept without any resistance, a sleep of one who knows they are to be delivered.

John sat with his jacket and coat loosely about him, creating a pocket of warm air that would resist the freezing will of the storm. He breathed slowly and deeply, using the least energy as he sat there and thought.

His life went before his eyes and he smiled gently as he saw his childhood. He recalled his family at picnics and peats, the joy of dancing competitively with his sister and rabbiting with his brother. And his teacher, Rachel MacDougall, was there in his mind's eye. Remembering their adventures with an otter he had befriended, and how he had written as much about her inelegant slide into the mud as much as he did about the otter. He smiled in gratitude for the freedom she opened in his mind. He had received so much.

John's expression did not change as he thought of his father, driven to madness by events he could not overcome. His heart welled with love for his father. He knew it was love that had driven his father to such lengths. He recalled the patient love of his mother and the winter expeditions to the mail boat as their major weekly outing. He gave thanks for the child, Catherine – fast asleep and warm within the insulation from the dead ewe. He offered respectful thanks to the ewe for enabling his little Catherine to live. He grieved at the wreckage earlier in his life when had turned himself into an alcoholic, not for what he did to himself but for the pain he had inflicted by rebuke and indifference on people who only loved him.

He dozed in the cold for only a moment. His mind kept him awake as he thought of the child Catherine and her mother and father. In the knowing of them they were as gifts to return him to himself. As morning light shafted through the darkness, he saw compassion as the saving grace of both himself and his fellow man. In that long night of freezing cold and driving blizzard his mind led him to these and many other paths and levels of his life. His suffering dissolved as his compassion grew.

By morning he arrived at full self-knowledge – a state of enlightenment that he remained in for the rest of his days. He had no regrets, was without fear, simply filled with a deep well of compassion and love that had always been there within him. He took his time sorting these insights with his mind that was now working with clarity about his life journey.

The blizzard had ended. Catherine was awake and alive and drew from the new strength and calmness that her elderly friend now possessed. He used his fisherman's knife to hack strips of fleece from the sheep to bind their feet and hands and wrap round her knees. Layers of fleece were thrust inside her cardigan and his jacket to keep them warm.

They left their small cave after Catherine gave a special prayer to the dead ewe that had saved her life. And a prayer to John, whom she loved so totally.

Now, they explored the land about them, looking for a path to follow. The snow had gently moulded Nature's indifference into a smooth quilt but he knew the way to the edge of the fell. They had been walking for an hour, helping and encouraging one another, when a shout turned them. There was Edgar, leaping through the snow to them, laughing and crying in relief that they were safe. He was haggard and wild eyed and near frozen but the two gave him life. He held Catherine to him and looked long and lovingly at John without speaking, taking his hand in his. He was overcome. He said very simply,

"I could not have lived if I had lost you both."

John embraced him slowly and all three had their arms about one another in their joy.

They were soon home. There was subdued excitement at the telling of the search and shelter. Breanne spent an hour gently holding John's feet in her warm hands to ease the chill from them. They were warmed and tired and grateful and closer than ever. And at Christmas they lifted their thanks to their God for deliverance and worshipped with calm intensity and deep joy.

John returned to his island, a fuller and wiser man. He opened himself to the ways of his own people. Many went to him, drawn by his softness and wisdom.

He made the small and ineffectual feel useful, redirected bitterness to joy. And loud, vicious men were gentled in his presence. There was an aura about him that transformed life's frailties and failings into a creative reality. His goodness and gentle acclaim were feared by some for he had power over men and knew that he did; thus he moved them to greater understanding and compassion.

Some resented his past indifference to them but on meeting with him, succumbed to his gentleness. They bore ill-concealed hurts that he healed, and wished him no harm.

But the men who feared him hated his goodness and sought his destruction. They could not find a way to it but they waited, jealously guarding their intent, carefully marking the time when they thought he would fall.

PART 4 – ALL MY RELATIONS: ANCIENT WISDOM

My long encounter with Ancient Wisdom enabled my heart and mind to expand in a manner that astonished me. I absorbed the significance of the Earth Mother and saw clearly how humanity neglected the basic respect for all that sustains us. Indigenous cycles of harvesting the Earth were based on an ethic of planning seven generations into the future. Such an ethic is not found in modern society. Indigenous wisdom the world over knows that protecting the Earth is primary to care for ourselves and all species. The era of Climate Crisis and Extinction is not a surprise to them.

My approach to life comes through experience, crises, difficulties and joys that may have common ground with many readers. I was gifted with mentors in the desert, training with sages in ashrams in India and the Ancient Wisdom of Indigenous cultures. My intensive training in different traditions enabled me to better understand the processes of transformation. There was a lot of mud in my seasons, yet that mud provided the necessary compost to cultivate surprisingly accurate insights. Thus, I was able to anticipate the hard core of Extinction by first of all developing Impermanence. And just why do I – do we – need all of this? It is so we may emerge as the new leaders for the 21st century.

I introduce Sacred Stalker in Chapter 10 and in Chapter 11: Medicine Mentors- my indigenous education. Chapter 12: The Transfer Particle is a futuristic story about Hopi mysticism for a new planet. Chapter 13: The Forest provides a short, sharp finale about my intentions.

Chapter Ten: Sacred Stalker

Several decades ago I became aware that I had a stalker. I would glance over my shoulder. Then feel a distinct presence that persisted in following me. White Eagle Woman, my shaman mentor, made it clear I was mistaken. This was no stalker. It was a woman from the 18th century, a medicine woman from the American Southwest. She was trying to bring powerful medicine gifts to me in the 21st century. She had a name – Trailing Sky Six Feathers. How did this come about?

When I was a young professor at Carleton University, I split my time between Ottawa, Canada, and the Hebrides in Scotland. I was trying to create an academic career and at the same time save a failing marriage. I was not doing a good job with either. I had a boat in the Hebrides, *An Dhoran* - a twenty six foot clinker built vessel, to enter the dangerous surrounding sea with tourists on board. One disastrous journey still scars my mind. It was from Eriskay to the north back to my home on the Island of Barra. The voyage across the stretch of sea separating Eriskay from Barra was uneventful. I started to navigate down the east coast of Barra and slammed in to an unanticipated storm and dense fog. It quickly morphed into gale force winds. It was impossible to return to Eriskay. There was no place to shelter on the east coast of Barra.

I knew the fierce sea conditions in the Minch, the stretch of sea that separates the islands from the mainland of Scotland, so I stayed close to the east coast of the island. The force of the storm was much more powerful than my twenty-five horsepower engine. Gale force winds swept the ocean swells to break over the prow of my boat. Sharp spray from the sea struck my face like pellets from a shotgun. I shielded my face with one arm to better see the huge waves coming right at the boat. My teenage son, Iain, used the boat hook to fend off the following dinghy from smashing into the stern of the boat. I felt myself entering a terrible, cold silence while braced at the wheel. There was no mind there, only an intuitive awareness of danger in this moment, then danger in the next moment. Navigation was just far enough away from the inshore spurs of rock jutting out like razors. The no-mind mariner at the wheel stood quietly muttering the 23rd Psalm, "I shall not want."

I turned *An Dhoran* through a narrow gap in an offshore rock spur. I caught a swell as it crested through the gap, spinning the wheel hard to port to avoid the ragged edge of another rock ledge, then quickly to starboard to find a more sheltered stretch of sea. I did not have that knowledge. I did not have that skill. It was beyond my capabilities. My mind did not operate, yet I had a seamless connection to a furious sea. A powerful instinctive knowledge took over as I felt an ethereal female guiding me through.

The frightened tourists sat inside the cabin for weight at the front end of the boat as the sea smashed into the creaking clinker boards. This extra ballast saved the timbers of our vessel from being split open. Something else had their hands on the wheel. The slow progress down the coastline of Barra continued under a mantle of desperate prayers. Later we limped slowly into the sheltered harbour of Castlebay. The mother of my children and then wife was there to gather Iain and take him home. The phone call that we were rounding the tip of Barra brought her to the dock at Castlebay harbour with blankets for my son and a fierce glare at me. We were not on good terms. The passengers disembarked with great relief.

I moored *An Dhoran* at her berth in the bay next to the Castle. The wind was dropping and the fog began to clear. I rowed to shore in the dinghy, then with ropes pulled it back to its mooring place. It sat there gently bobbing across from the Post Office and the small boat pier. I walked up the hill to the Castlebay Bar. Roddy, the barman, had already heard about the journey. News travels fast on the island. I placed two ten pound notes on the counter, the sum total of my earnings from a day of insanity on the sea.

"Roddy, this will cover me tonight."

Roddy's large hand held out a glass tumbler, which he filled with his best whisky.

"We'll not be taking your money my friend. Everyone is relieved you are back safely from Eriskay."

A long row of full whisky glasses appeared on the wooden bar I was wearily leaning against. My hands shook as I took the first glass of whisky from Roddy's huge fist. My mind was frozen. The cold silence told me it was not I who brought the boat home safely. At closing time I walked to my home, overlooking the bay. I could see the Castle and the islands to the south shrouded by the soft light from the quarter moon. It was calm and peaceful, nothing like the earlier hours on the sea. Sitting on the steps of my house, I went over in my mind this dangerous day. My reflections were savage, yielding ugly truths long buried.

I thought of the line of whiskies at the bar, a celebration of returning safe from the furious sea. There was nothing to celebrate. A rebuke was needed for my recklessness in endangering the lives of others, including my first born son. I could take no credit for bringing *An Dhoran* home. I thought of the tumultuous sea as a piercing dirty grey, the color of dying – just waiting for me. I was not in the right place internally and did not belong here. I had obscured this true confession with blind recklessness. The shrouds fell away and I could see just what I had allowed myself to become.

I was no heroic captain at the wheel, just stupid, reckless and displaced. I had to put an end to my madness on the sea. This was not my domain in life. This beautiful island in the Hebrides was not where I was to be. The stressful drain on time and energy travelling back and forth between Canada and the Isle of Barra was debilitating. It left me with zero life-force energy for the work I was destined to touch. I was merely surviving amidst the suffering of being totally misplaced. So down I went into the graceless oblivion that alcohol and depression permits.

I stood up slowly and stepped into my house. Still in the grip of that awful, chilling silence, I stretched out on the large sofa in the kitchen. My border collie Bruce crept over and rested his chin on my chest to provide comfort. I knew I had to change the course of my life and emerge from the swamp I had created. This deadly sea voyage was the signal to embark on a deep internal spiritual journey. They were not my hands on the wheel.

On my return to Canada after this brutal summer, I met White Eagle Woman at an elders gathering. Her air of quiet authority immediately struck me. She looked into me deeply and saw that I needed help. She had been instructed by her ancestors to train me and it began straight away with an eight day vision quest, prelude to a thirty year period of training and healing under her guidance. This allowed the mosaic of the past to reveal itself. She identified Trailing Sky Six Feathers for me and revealed the guardian role held by her. White Eagle Woman also taught me how to create a medicine wheel in my mind. I was always to start by bringing into my mind the ancient shaman from the East, then the South, West and North in succession, finally to bring in the ancient shaman from the Centre. She told me to see this as a map in my mind. I was instructed to call forth the animal guides I had personally experienced, again starting from the East. I had experienced many animal guides and told her so.

White Eagle Woman retorted with some exasperation:

"Choose the most powerful ones, dammit!"

With that cryptic encouragement, I chose mountain lion in the East, moose in the South, elk in the West and medicine bear in the North, with dolphin and whale below and the great eagles above. The space at the centre of the mental medicine wheel was the conduit for me to dialog with Trailing Sky Six Feathers – but only when connection to the sacred mystery was intact.

When I died in her arms in 1777 she vowed to find me in the future. She refused to give up on how dense I was in present time. Through her insistent guidance, my karma was reversed. The internal battles ceased. I learned to navigate past and present

140

life experiences over four centuries. The medicine gifts from her required that I nurture skills to use them wisely. A clear mosaic of experiences stretching back to 1777 was in my mind.

Once the Vision Quest with White Eagle Woman was complete, I carefully built the medicine wheel in my mind and spoke to Trailing Sky about the sea journey.

"Trailing Sky, was it you that brought my boat safely home?" I already knew the answer.

"You were there on all the other dangerous voyages – were you not Trailing Sky?" I said softly to her, affirming her guardian presence.

She responded after a long pause:

"I had to keep you alive, your son too, for he receives the Torch after your passing. I kept you alive when you almost lost your right arm in a foolish fight in Vancouver. I also kept you alive when you were dying in India."

Flashing through my mind were all the moments when death had faced me in this lifetime. She had always been there whenever my life was at risk and brought me through to safety. I took our dialog to another level,

"When I die, will you be there? What will happen to you?"

Her voice was soft and precise.

"When you die, I will be the last portion of your consciousness to dissolve. Before that moment of dissolution I will guide both of us as one integrated mind into the next adventure."

I was stunned into a long silence and refrained from asking about the next adventure. Trailing Sky Six Feathers is not an illusion, a projection I am attached to. She constitutes all that is crystal clear and wise within me - the ultimate Muse. I stayed very quiet until it was late in the night. I knew she was listening in to my thoughts. Just before midnight she quietly said to me,

"You have transformed all that you brought in with you and suffered from in this life. The person who stumbled blindly through the first part of your life is not the Ian walking through the second part of life. In India, Arizona, France, the Canadian wilderness and around the world you went to extraordinary lengths to deal with karma. You changed course and now have freedom and alignment. There were so many severe experiences, but you responded by moving in a spiritual direction. You touched universal threads that allowed me to keep my promise from 1777. And we are both grateful for that."

I could feel her smile expand along with my own. I placed my hands together with great reverence and offered a deep bow of gratitude to Trailing Sky Six Feathers. Namaste...

Chapter Eleven: Medicine Mentors

White Eagle Woman

It was during a gathering of elders in 1978 that I first met White Eagle Woman. She saw how troubled, dense and unaware I was.

The introduction to White Eagle Woman enabled my disjointed education and experience with the Indigenous domain of mysticism to slowly evolve into a seamless pattern rather than remain as random knots stretching across an abyss.

She was a heavy set woman with a round face and long black hair, but it was her universal presence that got my full attention. She rarely smiled, but when she did it illuminated the entire room as her dark eyes lit up with mirth.

I was very fortunate to be in her hands. She was the first of four incredible medicine people who provided me with shamanic training and teachings over the next three decades. White Eagle Woman directed the shamanic process of my healing from childhood sexual abuse. This allowed the mosaic of the past to start revealing itself.

Shamans and medicine people from far and wide came to consult with White Eagle Woman. Elders from the Amazon would come to see her. She was a holder of the Midewiwin lineage, a secret tradition of medicine people which stretched far and wide across the Americas.

At that first encounter at the elder's gathering she told me about a Vision Quest on her reserve in Sault Ste. Marie in south western Ontario. I was to be there, as she had received instructions from her ancestors to train me. That was enough for my attendance.

The eight day Vision Quest began and finished with a sweat lodge. In between were six days of fasting, prayer and ceremony in the wilderness. White Eagle Woman located me in a small grove of birch and oak trees and I had to stay within a strictly designated area. The other seven participants in the Vision Quest were located in a different part of the forest, distant and unseen.

I found some level ground for my tarp and strung it over a frame, built from what I could find within the grove. I placed my four coloured ribbons – yellow, black, white, red - at each of the four directions, also for the realms of above and below. The ribbons had awareness meanings for the Vision Quest. One of the oak trees became the symbolic stem of my pipe. The bowl of the pipe was a clamshell with tobacco in it. As the sun moved the tree's shadow, I had to be alert and move the clamshell in the same direction around the base of the tree. The symbolic pipe honoured the ancestors..

I was very still and silent, observing my territory's nuances, the leaves, smells, insects and rain, all while in a constant state of prayer and thanksgiving. White Eagle Woman located herself in a trailer close by for anyone who needed guidance. She indicated that a medicine bear would visit one of us and to report that to her.

Time passed in a seamless flow, scarcely existing before we gathered for the final sweat lodge once the Vision Quest was over. There was such a stillness, even when it rained, one day evolved into the next as I went deeper within.

On coming off the land, a surprise awaited. I had to consume a half cup of blueberries and then drink vast quantities of a foul tasting concoction created by White Eagle Woman. This was a cleansing medicine to make me throw up the blueberries. It was quite disgusting. Especially for me, as it took a long time before I vomited up the blueberries. White Eagle Woman's comment to me was terse. She pursed her lips and looked at me quizzically:

"Hmmm – you're holding on tight to resist the truth you need to know!"

I had no idea what she was referring to.

White Eagle Woman asked about the medicine bear. Nobody reported experiencing it. In exasperation she turned to me and announced that she had seen the medicine bear visit me twice. What did I remember? I recalled dreaming about a tall, gangly and somewhat goofy creature that was not a bear to my mind. I had also noticed the creature on another day, out of the corner of my eye, sitting next to the sacred oak tree. White Eagle Woman immediately threw tobacco on the fire to absolve my ignorant gaffe and instructed me that a medicine bear can take on many forms. The goofy creature was the most receptive one for an idiot like me.

Though the medicine bear had been easy on me, White Eagle Woman was certainly not. She chastised my lack of insight while we were all in the sweat lodge. Later on, in private, she quietly revealed the door that had been opened wide due to the medicine bear experience.

The visit was to assess whether I was capable of receiving medicine gifts from the past – clarity of seeing, avoiding harm and connecting to other dimensions.

White Eagle Woman also identified the female entity that was trying to come through to me, as a medicine woman from the American southwest, before white settlement. She even named her: Trailing Sky Six Feathers. She then taught me how to place in my mind the sacred medicine wheel with particular focus on the central circle. That was the location through which Trailing Sky and I could communicate. And furthermore, I was to immediately use the mental medicine wheel to talk to her. I did so, as instructed.

On a daily basis I followed White Eagle Woman's instructions. I would come to a stop, look deeply and dialog with this feminine seed of knowledge in my consciousness.

I listened in the silence to Trailing Sky's feminine wisdom to address issues and questions. This became my fieldwork of life, observation and new understanding of consciousness through the eyes of the internal feminine. Silence and skillful deep looking were certainly important, yet I knew that dialog with Trailing Sky was the key.

I made diary entries with my questions and dilemmas, doubts and misgivings then waited quietly for a reply from within. I wrote with respect, love and gratitude and anticipated counsel to arise from inside. It was frequently not what I expected, hence my faith in its integrity. My own hopes of particular answers never happened, so my mind was not clouded by ego.

Shortly after she had taught me how to create a mental medicine wheel, White Eagle Woman asked me to work with her in an intense series of journeying. This was a process of guiding me while in an altered state of consciousness. I was surprised by the invitation. She also ensured that I trained with other shamans in journeying, so I could eventually create a form that would be acceptable for non-indigenous people. With her, the final journey of five sessions cleared the dross and fears I still carried from my lived in life. At the same time, it brought the awesome significance of Trailing Sky through to me.

Remembering

"Deep breaths rattle in and out of my chest. My legs are shaking, sweat pours down my face and body. My eyes are stinging but I can't wipe the sweat away. If I do I'll lose my balance.

I keep my arms extended and close my eyes. I stand there, suspended in time and space, my breathing calms. My legs and arms stop trembling and the sweat is no longer coursing down my body. I open my eyes. Several shafts of light penetrate the darkness. I am standing on one strand of a giant spider web stretching across an abyss, from one side of the cavern to the other. This strand is my sole source of support – a gift from Grandmother Spider. I feel the fibers of the strand beneath each foot as they cradle and balance my slow progress. Eternity seems to pass as I inch along, until finally my left foot comes down on solid rock.

My heart pounds as I look behind for a fleeting, dreadful moment. I peer into the deep, dark abyss plunging forever below the hard rock platform I now stand on. The grip of the fibers still pulses through my feet as I stand on firm earth.

I breathe deeply to steady my nerves and without hesitation walk along the rocky incline leading away from the abyss. Ghouls, creatures and phantoms of all kinds move through the cavern but I walk with determination away from the danger that had entrapped me.

The shock of sunlight blinds me for a moment then I see a verdant valley stretching ahead. A trail leads to a river where I take off my clothes and submerge myself in the crisp, cold water. The danger I carried from the abyss washes away. I warm myself on a rock and then dress. There is a pair of shoes in my leather satchel. I slip them on.

I follow the river in the direction of the sun. Mallard ducks preen at the water's edge with their ducklings and a kingfisher sits patiently on a branch overhanging a deep, still pool. Sunlight filters through the trees and the light dances on the water, shimmering and moving with every swirl and eddy.

The river leads me to its source – a beautiful lake cradled by high snow-capped mountains. At the end of the lake I see a cow moose with her calf at the water's edge.

In the distance wolves call to one another, and there are two rabbits beside me. A doe and two fawns walk slowly and tentatively from the forest into the sunlight, unafraid of my presence.

Skylarks hover motionless in the sky then descend to earth with their lilting song. Being close to all these creatures fills me with a feeling of well-being, but I was compelled to move on from this peaceful spot.

As I stand to leave, a huge golden eagle circles above me - my guardian. Tall pines mark the edge of the forest and I follow a path to a large clearing.

147

A fire flickers beside the flat rock in the centre of the clearing and there is a woman tending it. She is beautiful, tall with long black hair loosely braided on either side of her oval face. In her crafted buckskin garment she moves as gracefully as a deer. She stops putting wood on the fire and stands tall, watching me. Her dark eyes gravely observe my progress to the center of the clearing where I stand in front of her. I knew instantly that she was Trailing Sky Six Feathers. She tells me:

> "We have been expecting you, though wondered if you would get through the dangers of the abyss. The Ancient Shaman of the West is waiting to talk to you. Take the path ahead of you and follow it to the mountain."

The path leads towards the mountains. I feel transported to a valley where there is a small cedar building ahead. The heavy wooden front door is wide open and as I enter, a deep melodious voice greets me.

"Welcome, it is about time that we met."

Oil lamps cast a glow over simple wooden furnishings with animal skins thrown over them. Spears and traps adorn the walls. There is a central fire and an altar on the east side. I smell the aroma of burning sage and feel the intense sacred nature of this abode.

In front of me is a magnificent old man dressed in a splendid embroidered buckskin tunic and trousers. His hair is white, as is his trimmed moustache and beard. His dark skin makes his smile all the more dazzling. He is easily six feet tall with an athletic body underneath the bearskin robe thrown over one shoulder. All of this vitality seems at odds with his obviously advancing years, his weathered skin evidence of his life's journey. His dark eyes penetrate every aspect of my being as he regards me for a long moment.

"Come sit with me. We will share some tea."

I make myself comfortable on a bench by the fireplace, feeling at peace as we sip tea together in silence.

"There is someone who wishes to meet with you. She passed on to the other side many years ago. Yet she still carries a great burden of sorrow. And that sorrow has to do with you. Are you prepared to meet your favorite Aunt?"

"You mean my Aunt Ruby?"

He nods and there is my Aunt Ruby sitting opposite me on another bench. She is just as I remember her, wearing a fashionable pant suit, her greying hair pulled back in a bun to display the beauty of her cheekbones and elegant face. When I was seriously ill as a young teen, she took care of me and nursed me back to health. I suffered from a general malaise that my family's doctor diagnosed as rheumatic fever – but it was not that at all. Had I been born into a society steeped in shamanism, the elders would have seen that this was a shamanic illness, announcing that I was ready for training. But I was not born into such an alert society, and so my shamanic training was postponed until my middle years. But she looked troubled and sad. It hurt to see my aunt so distraught and miserable. Very softly I ask her,

"Tell me why you seem so troubled Aunt Ruby?"

"Oh my Ian, there is no *seem* about it. I knew, as did your other aunties, about the sexual abuse you endured at the hands of our second cousin, when he was on leave from the army. We all felt that we had failed to protect you. We took some solace in that you seemed not to remember. So we kept quiet about it, keeping it as a family secret. But I have carried this deep suffering into the grave and beyond, my sisters and your parents too. I am so sorry Ian for not protecting you."

I sit patiently, waiting for her sobbing to subside, and smiled gently to her.

"My dearest Aunt Ruby – please stop your tears. I became aware of the abuse and its effects on me as I got older. In my middle years I had wonderful help from powerful healers and shamans and was able to release the energy of abuse so it no longer harms me as it once did. I even found

forgiveness for the man responsible – your second cousin. If I can let go of the suffering, then surely you can do the same. And your sisters and my parents can let go of any grief they still carry. None of you need to suffer on the other side."

Her crying stops. She collects herself and in a tremulous voice Aunt Ruby asks,

"Is this really true Ian? You are not just saying this to placate me? I could not bear that."

"The pain, suffering and violence from the abuse are no longer with me. It is only logical that it is no longer with you. Don't you think so? You must share this news with your sisters and my parents on the other side."

She nods, silent for a while, pre-occupied with her thoughts and suffering. Then she smiles her great broad grin.

"You were always my favorite nephew – the little philosopher. I remember our conversations about insects, God and the universe. When you stayed in my home when you were so ill – that was one of the happiest six months of my life."

Her eyes light up. Ruby's sorrow had been lifted and in an instant she is gone.

The Ancient Shaman of the West, who observed our exchange, looks at me with those penetrating dark eyes,

"This is what you came to do Ian. It is now time for you to go back."

"Come back Ian." The voice calling to me grows more and more insistent. *"Come back."*

And so I travelled back. I was lying down on a bear skin with a pillow under my head. White Eagle Woman, medicine woman of the Ojibwa, sat in her armchair - very carefully observing me on the floor of her home.

"I will help you stand up as you will be shaky after that journey. And brush you down with an eagle wing. Then you can sit down on the sofa and tell me every part of your journey. First – drink this glass of water."

With one hand on my shoulder she brushed me from head to toe with the eagle wing in her other hand and I felt the strength of eagle medicine enter my body and mind, knowing I was coming to rest in a stable state. I sat down on the brown sofa and White Eagle Woman listened intently as I spoke, occasionally asking me to repeat and clarify the sequence of events I was describing. She pointed out several vital components of the journey that I had missed. She was very thoughtful once I finished speaking. I respected her silence. Then she looked at me shrewdly, as if through new eyes.

"This journey had more than I ever expected of you. Grandmother Spider rarely shows herself as a helper. Her job is to spin the threads of the Universe, yet she took time out to build that web across the abyss for you. It is only thanks to her that you could walk out of the darkness of the cavern and begin your intended journey. You were totally unaware of how much her gift means and of the other gifts placed on your journey – and that includes Trailing Sky's appearance at the clearing. She has been brought to your full attention. But what sticks with me the most right now is that you offered gifts to your Aunt Ruby so that her suffering could diminish."

She paused, tapping her feet on the floor in concentration, and considered very carefully her next words to me:

"The Ancient Shaman of the West is very pleased with your compassion and courage. And so am I."

With that rare acknowledgement, White Eagle Woman stomped off to the kitchen to make tea – leaving me to wonder about what else I had missed and still did not understand. This was the state of unknowing from where I began the process of remembering.

Susan Tatoosh

In 1990, I took a sabbatical leave from my job at Carleton University in Ottawa. In addition to teaching an Anthropology course at the University of British Columbia in Vancouver, I was conducting energy and healing workshops in the city. This led to my offering a retreat in the high plateau area of southern Colorado, near Crestone. Quite a few people had signed up for this but all fell away except one: Susan Tatoosh, elder and shaman of the Shuswap First Nation. She was very quiet spoken with a gentle smile that lit up her features. She carried her slim frame with great elegance. The power within her was largely concealed, as I later found out when I became the butt of her exasperation.

She knew that her ancestors were instructing her to guide me to realizations I had long ago buried. The retreat turned into a major learning experience for me, as Susan led me to deeper revelations not the other way around as I had expected. We spent time in meditation and ceremony. The arid desert scrub of the high plateau, cut through by small streams, was our backyard. Wherever we walked there was always a gathering of eagles. I did not notice this until Susan pointed out our recurring company. One morning after breakfast she called to me,

"Ian, there is someone here to speak with you."

I went to the door. There was no-one there, or on the pathway.

"Who?" "Where?"

She pointed to a large golden eagle on the scrubland close to the house.

"He is there waiting for you."

I slowly walked over, approached the eagle and squatted down.

"Do you hear anything?" The elder was right behind me.

"No."

"Stop thinking. Empty your mind. Do you hear anything?"

"No."

"He called you by a name you should remember. Did you hear?

"No."

There was a long pause from the elder. She continued,

"You're so useless Ian. From the way you are squatting down your name should be Shits with Eagles."

In exasperation she slapped me on the back of the head and stormed back to the house and watched me from the doorway. I slowly rose to my feet and waited for the eagle to fly. He stayed there right in front of me. Then I felt, or heard him communicate, that I should go to the elder. I did. She was still steamed with me.

"Don't you realize yet Ian? You were here before and could speak with eagles and other creatures? That's what the eagle told me and you got nothing. I will name you rightly as Shits with Eagles. You are so stuck in your own shit in your mind"

I offered to Susan that I had heard the eagle speak as I stood up – to return to the elder. She put her hands on her hips, still fuming:

"Progress at last. Maybe he will come to you in dreamtime and you had better tell me. For now, get out there and listen without any thought in that shit laden mind of yours. Breathe slowly as I have taught you. Stand apart from all notions. Wait. Listen."

Still I heard nothing, sensed nothing – I just looked at this magnificent creature.

"Speaks with Eagles, we have been waiting for you."

Where did that voice come from? Was this some kind of trick? I turned round to see Susan smiling. Was she a ventriloquist playing with me? She gestured that I turn my gaze and attention to the eagle. He was preening his feathers, still there within ten feet of me. I took a small step forward and kneeled down so our eyes were on the same level. Not that eagles smile, but it felt as though this one was amused by my discomfort as I knelt on stones and a small cactus. I found it strange that I had sensed the name "Speaks with Eagles." That was a name bestowed upon me by an Algonquin elder ten years ago in 1980 during a sweat lodge ceremony to reconnect humanity to the Earth Mother. Susan Tatoosh knew about this ceremony and the naming. It was the source of her scornful sarcasm.

The eagle and I stayed like that immobile for an endless moment.

"We protect and guide your direction."

The voice in my head was deep and resonant. I felt myself going into a sort of trance and wondered if I was hallucinating. What had Susan put in my food at breakfast? Really stupid things I thought of. The great eagle was patient and waited for my thoughts to fade away.

"We will come to you in ways you cannot know. We are at the pinnacle of the medicine wheel that becomes sanctuary for you."

What medicine wheel? Aaaaah, the one that White Eagle Woman instructed me to create in my mind of course. I get it. Then quickly I came back to stillness, ignoring the ache in my leg muscles and the cactus needle in my left knee. For long moments I gave myself up to this beautiful eagle, not understanding too much at all. Then he gathered himself and launched into flight. I watched him as he flew with huge wing beats over the scrubland towards the southern hills of the Rockies surrounding Crestone. Even when he was out of sight, I just stayed there.

Then there were Susan's hands gently on my shoulders.

"You can stand up now."

My left knee was bleeding. She led me to the house and applied ice to the knee, which had become quite swollen. She had heard everything and knew I was now open to being tutored by her wisdom. Susan Tatoosh, elder of the Shuswap nation, educated me about Eagle Medicine, as her ancestors had instructed.

154

Grandfather William Commanda

Grandfather William Commanda, spiritual elder of the Algonquin nation, taught me about the legends of the Seven Fires Prophecy. He was revered throughout Quebec and Ontario, and created The Circle of All Nations organization some forty years ago.

It was inclusive, as the name implies, and a very unpopular step with many aboriginal groups who had suffered greatly from oppression by the wider society.

His vision, however, was clear - to create a global centre for all peoples at the sacred Chaudiere Falls in the city of Ottawa, based on models of healing and reconciliation long established in aboriginal culture. The plans and architecture were carefully drawn together and simply await implementation.

Grandfather had a welcoming spirit and a twinkle of humour in his kind eyes. He was open to everyone who wished to spend time with him and share his wisdom.

He taught me what he and other Native American spiritual leaders believe, that present day humanity has entered the Seventh Fire - a time for hard choices, to either remain on the same destructive course or incubate a major change in consciousness so the Eighth Fire can be ignited. This is an internal Fire for basic human goodness to prevail.

The Seven Fires Prophecy is meant for all peoples, to encourage a new generation to fearlessly come together and create a society based on earth wisdom and harmony. I was told by Grandfather that it invokes an end to bloodshed and suffering, the beginning of forgiving and reconciliation.

He was the holder of the Seven Fires Prophecy Wampum Belt until he died in 2011. The belt was created in 1400 CE and encodes the potential evolution from the Seventh Fire to the Eighth Fire.

I discovered from him that the prophecy was both a warning and an opportunity for reconciliation and change.

Grandfather was a formidable figure and influenced me greatly in the writing of *Failsafe: Saving the Earth From Ourselves.* He provided a generous testimonial. I drew upon the wisdom of the elders to show that human beings are programmed literally with a Failsafe, which will ultimately kick in, unleashed by our very will to survive.

The Failsafe I was describing referred to the necessary incorporation of the Eighth Fire into everyday life.

Grandfather was also a trickster with a wicked sense of humour. He warned me, with a hint of mischief, that I would receive a visit from the Thunder Beings that would scare the hell out of me and totally confuse everyone else.

Pine Gate Mindfulness Community in Ottawa, where I am the Zen teacher, had for some years participated in an annual sweat lodge ceremony. Just before 2004's winter set in, we entered into an extraordinary *inipi* experience.

On a rain swept day, nine members of the Pine Gate community travelled to a remote location in the Gatineau Hills to meet the lodge keeper, Roy Barnes. Grandfather had first introduced me to him at the sweat lodge I was invited to participate in to reconnect humanity with the Earth Mother. Roy was the fire-keeper for that ceremony on Victoria Island next to the sacred Chaudiere Falls, the location for Grandfather's vision to establish a centre for the Circle of All Nations.

Roy was trained in the Lakota Sioux tradition and was also a Sun Dance leader. We were joined by four Dene Chiefs from the Northwest Territories as well as by five members of Roy's First Nations community. I felt these two sets of nine as one body of eighteen.

Despite the relentless rain, the fire heated the grandfather rocks beautifully.

The ceremony began with blessings and purification. In the first round I was asked to speak about my work for peace and reconciliation and to extend a welcome to the Dene chiefs from the far north of Canada.

One of the chiefs replied and honoured me for setting in motion the reconciliation between traditions and cultures. There was an auspicious energy present from the get-go that soon turned into a startling reality.

In the third round, as the men offered prayers for the Earth, thunderclaps exploded overhead and a lightning bolt struck the sweat lodge, travelling underground into the fire pit. No one was hurt or injured, but we all felt the ground shake underneath us like a mini earthquake.

After the completion of the fourth round, we emerged from the sweat lodge quite shaken yet knew something awesome had taken place. The fire keeper tending to the rocks and wood for the fire recounted how the entire sky turned a bright yellow when the lightning bolt struck the sweat lodge.

In the weeks and months that followed, Roy and the Dene chiefs consulted with elders and medicine people about the events of this *inipi* ceremony. They were told that this was a Thunder Beings lodge, a mark of respect for whoever had been honoured inside the *inipi*.

Most elders had only heard of this in legend and offered honour to whoever received this blessing from the Thunder Beings. When this was told to me, I placed the honour on the Dene Chiefs and the lodge keeper. They stated firmly that this was for me, though we had all been marked by this auspicious visit from the Thunder Beings.

Roy later related to me that the medicine people and Sun Dancers across the country honoured the work I do by keeping me in their prayers so that I would be protected. I was humbled by this unexpected source of support.

Dawson's Desert Legacy

Dawson was a wisdom holder of many traditions – Ojibwa, Hopi, Lakota and the Native American Church. He was a legendary figure in Central Arizona and left a lasting impression on everyone he met.

I have encountered many people at conferences and talks all over North America and when it emerges that I have spent a considerable amount of time in Central Arizona desert country, I am always asked if I know a man named Dawson.

He had met all kinds of people in his capacity as a guide and teacher. Yet his attention and presence never wavered in its intensity as he welcomed all into his orbit of wisdom and patience.

I first met him in 1987 on a day-long ethno-botany field trip he offered in the Sonoran desert region of Central Arizona. I was the only person to turn up, yet this did not deter him.

He generously extended his knowledge of plants and hidden sources of water in the scrubland of the Sonora desert.

His field trip skirted ancient medicine wheels created centuries ago. He talked about plant cycles within the teachings of the medicine wheel both for ceremony and healing. His mentorship has always meant a great deal to me, especially his instruction of how to build a medicine wheel.

Dawson was a slender yet muscular man in his sixties, though he seemed much older. His manner was slow and deliberate, gentle but firm though his light blue eyes carried a steely glint. He loved movies and would always sit in the cinema until the end of the credits, the last person to leave. Eyes closed, he made a point of downloading the full feeling of the film. It was the same with people, animals and the desert. He brought a sense of gentle intensity and intimacy to every relationship.

The initial connection from that first field trip and movie experience warmed into a friendship.

One evening in Sedona, two years after our initial meeting, I received a call from him. He asked if I would pick him up two hours before dawn the next morning.

"Wear hiking boots," he said.

I drove in the early morning dark to Cornville and found him waiting outside his house. I followed his directions to take various forestry roads leading to a reserve on the northern fringe of the Sonora desert.

After parking, we hiked for approximately thirty minutes into the desert through a scrubland trail. It was still dark when he gestured that we should stop.

We shared a flask of coffee and the intense silence of the desert, interrupted only by the scurry of small wildlife.

n the dark of morning just before dawn Dawson gestured for me to look in the direction of three large cacti directly in front of us. The sun rose and I could vaguely make out the flowers opening. Then Dawson pointed them out. They were absolutely stunning in their unreal beauty, ranging from yellow to dark violet. We sat there for over an hour, appreciating their beauty, as the morning sun rose.

"You had to see this before you travelled home to Canada," were his only spoken words.

The morning heat was suddenly broken by a fierce hail storm. We put our packs over our heads and ran quickly to the shelter of the nearest rocky outcrop. The storm lasted ten minutes although the stones were not small, making quite an impact on any unprotected area of the body.

Dawson looked at me strangely:

"That sure is some kind of acknowledgement from the past, and it ain't for me. What have you been up to Mister Ian?" Dawson asked.

I just shrugged, as I had no intimations of cause.

159

We walked in silence to where I had parked the car. The hailstones were not to be found beyond a hundred yard perimeter of where we had been sitting.

"Beats the hell out of me, though I reckon you will have some building to do back in Canada," said Dawson cryptically, as he peered at me out of the corner of his eye.

These were the last words I heard him speak. As was his custom we drove in silence. He got out of the car by his property, waved once and was gone.

On a later journey in 1992 to that region of Arizona, when enquiring about him, I discovered to my dismay that he had been killed in a car accident outside Phoenix. I was deeply saddened by this loss, thinking about all that he had so patiently taught me.

I drove to where I had last walked with him, to pay my respects to this extraordinary spiritual teacher, remembering the way there, almost without thinking.

It was not the time for the cacti to flower but I treasured once again the gift he had shown me. I wondered who he had passed on his vast knowledge to, then realized suddenly that he had passed on a great deal to me about medicine wheel lore and construction.

Dawson was a spiritual guide and had taken me through many shamanic journeys. The hailstone storm was no longer a mystery to me, rather an early prompt. What I had received from him was put into place in the hermitage where I lived, in the Gatineau Forest in Quebec.

Over a period of five months in the spring and summer of 1994 I experienced very intensive shamanic journeys with an Algonquin shaman that I prepared for through fasting, meditation and sexual abstinence.

On five separate journeys I met and dialogued with ancient shamans from the East, the South, the West, the North and finally to the ancient shaman of the Center.

I figured at first that this was an experience with five facets of the same archetypal material from my deep unconscious, though there were major surprises I had not anticipated. Each shaman created distinctive unconscious energy within me, interconnected to the other four.

In each journey I was always met by the same beautiful female figure, who then led me to the ancient shaman. I knew instantly who she was – Trailing Sky Six Feathers. Dawson had repeatedly told me that the sacred feminine would eventually emerge as a Muse for me, and there she was. White Eagle Woman had anticipated this earlier in my training with intensive shamanic journeys with her.

At my hermitage in the middle of Gatineau Park Forest in Quebec, I had a small circle of large stones in my front yard with beautiful ferns growing at the center. I had an overwhelming compulsion that summer of 1994 to build a medicine wheel with this circle of stones as the interior circle. I had been taught by Dawson the appropriate mind-state and procedure of respect to construct a medicine wheel.

Dawson had instructed me intensely in Arizona about the central circle of the medicine wheel. It could only be truly experienced when connection to the sacred mystery was intact. The four cardinal directions, East, West, South and North, were the organizing axis for this ultimate fusion, represented by the ferns over which I took such care. It had sunk into my intellect but now reached my heart.

I constructed the medicine wheel with the assistance of two friends who shared my respect and training. We carried out the appropriate ritual, and worked with reverence on a very hot and humid summer's day. The silence that settled on all three of us spoke of something happening inside and around us while creating this architecture of incredible grace, power and beauty. The stones for the medicine wheel came from my garden and the surrounding forest, the hard granite of the Canadian Shield, part of the very ground where the medicine wheel was being built.

After filling the four quadrants of the medicine wheel with fresh garden soil, we contemplated what had been created. I realized its connection to my five shamanic journeys in the spring and summer.

The cardinal points of the wheel and its center were a reflection of the five ancient shamans I had journeyed to meet and the ferns at the centre were an appropriate symbol for the feminine muse that delivered me to each shaman. The medicine wheel was a symbolic map of my internal experience. I was re-inventing the wheel from my journeys to meet the five Ancient Shamans, yet also ensured that the beautiful ferns remained intact at the centre of the medicine wheel.

I started to smile at how this medicine lore and knowledge had gradually seeped into my consciousness from Dawson. His overarching influence had prepared me for the journeys to the five shamans. I could feel his intense blue eyes watching me at this moment and perhaps he permitted himself a smile too.

It was his instructions I followed for my medicine wheel. He had known that I would eventually understand the wheel and the space at the center as the locale where I would seek counsel from the sacred feminine - the beautiful ferns. Just as White Eagle Woman had taught me – to communicate with Trailing Sky Six Feathers.

Chapter Twelve: The Transfer Particle

Manny Fredericks was of Hopi descent, a brilliant astrophysicist with a distinctive mystical flair.

He had published a provocative treatise on parallel universes and combined astrophysics with traditional indigenous ways of placing energy and intent from one universe to another.

Manny alleged that the mystical component mirrored the Transfer Molecule – a crossover particle that science had long sought in its understanding of co-existing universes. The elusive particle was believed to have properties that enabled it to cross from one universe to another and that such penetration could alter energy patterns.

Dr. Tom Hagen was intrigued when he read the manuscript. He was the chef-de-mission of the International Space Agency's PRIME 3 project to locate a suitable planet, as habitation on Earth became increasingly compromised.

The International Space Agency had established research stations orbiting Mars and on Jupiter's moon Europa. Station One at Jupiter was the key construction.

In 2080 probes - PRIME 1 and 2 - from Jupiter were launched into the heliosphere through a wormhole into interstellar space.

In a neighboring galaxy they located a planet with two moons in an ecliptic plane with a dozen planets orbiting around a massive sequence star, the sun for this system.

The planet had a liquid hydrosphere similar to Earth.

The probes sent back information identifying distinct zones from tropics to polar with evidence of oceans, forests and mountains. No sign of habitation was revealed.

Both probes identified a dense particle field in the upper stratosphere of the planet, similar to a Van Allen belt. The long-term plan was for Jupiter One to serve as a way station to ferry pioneers to the new planet.

Tom immediately tracked down Manny through his advanced optic phone. He explained the PRIME 3 space project and was surprised to learn that Manny was aware of it. Their conversation focused on the mystical component alluded to in Manny's treatise. They were both excited in their sharing and blending of thoughts. The conversation ended with an invitation for Tom to travel to the Hopi Mesas in Northern Arizona. Tom jumped at the opportunity and days later he was at Phoenix International Airport.

It was hot and dusty inside and outside the airport. The expansion of desert had penetrated from the Sonora right into the city. Manny was waiting for him. He was tall for a Hopi, almost six feet. He wore a white T-shirt with 'DON'T WORRY BE HOPI' emblazoned in black across the front. His long black hair was pulled into a pony tail and his chiseled face lit up with a smile when he saw Tom walking towards him, extending his hand in greeting.

There was a helicopter from the Space Agency to fly them directly to the Hopi pueblos. On the flight Manny explained that his people had largely evacuated their villages with the encroaching desert eroding pasture for their herds of sheep and cattle. Yet one pueblo was still inhabited by elders who kept the ceremonial cycle alive, and indeed developed it further to anticipate Earth collapse. There was a cadre of supporters taking care of them. His grandmother had called in the elderly Keepers of the Energies. They were patiently waiting Tom and Manny's arrival.

On the flight to Northern Arizona, Manny provided a brief overview of Hopi cosmology.

Tom was intrigued as he listened intently, fascinated at the year round ceremonial cycle that challenged humans to develop through intricate and complex rituals.

Generations of anthropologists who had researched the Hopi were baffled by this intricacy, not realizing that the obstacle to understanding was their lack of mystical grounding.

Manny presented a rhythm of life through the chasm of disbelief, feeling certain that he and Tom would be instrumental in closing the lack of knowledge. He confided that he and Tom had already been "seen" by the elders, who were waiting for the cosmic order to unfold.

Manny asked Tom through the headphones,

"Do you have the co-ordinates for the new planet's location? My grandmother will need to know that very precisely."

Tom did have the location specs, but wondered why an elderly Hopi elder would need them. He did not voice his query, but Manny picked up on the concern.

"Tom, do not be fooled by my grandmother when you meet her. She has Master's degrees in both mathematics and quantum physics. She has already made it clear to me what she needs from you. She may look like a traditional elder, but there is much more to her than that."

Tom smiled as Manny provided further information about this formidable woman.

"When she graduated from MIT her professors begged her to continue to a Ph.D., as they had rarely encountered a mind like hers. She declined, as her life trajectory was ceremonial, creating new vistas for harmony with what she knew from science and her tradition. Her entire thesis was grounded in ceremonial principles and built with impeccable logic to move the boundaries of understanding. She provided a new level of expression and intent and was the instigator for me to write the article that brought you here. You will find her an extraordinary woman."

Tom nodded and changed the focus by asking Manny whether he was choosing science over ceremonial. Manny gave Tom a broad grin.

"With a grandmother like mine, there was no choice to make. While I am devoted to science and love it, I do know where my starting point is. And if I ever forget, I have that steel trap mind of my grandmother to deal with."

Manny dug into his pocket and pulled out an envelope addressed to Tom.

"My grandmother has a message for you. Here it is."

Tom carefully opened the envelope and read the neat handwriting.

My grandson is integral to the ceremony we will create. It is necessary for him to accompany you on the journey to the new planet. He has the knowledge to provide a foundation for your enterprise. You will need him.

This note was not a request. Tom also intuited that he was about to face the largest leap of faith in his entire life. He carefully tucked the note inside his jacket pocket and asked Manny to provide some details of the ceremony being prepared by the Hopi elders. Manny composed himself and placed his mind in his grandmother's and began to speak the words she would use.

"My grandmother asked me to wait until you posed this question. There are four Sacred Keepers, and that includes her. They have already prepared the kiva for a new departure in their ceremonial cycle. The kiva is a large underground ceremonial chamber, like a womb in the Earth body. It enables life and death to enfold in seamless continuity. It is built of stone and placed in the central plaza of the pueblo in accordance with the four directions, North, East, South and West. The ceremony will take place in the underground chamber. It has a sunken fire pit in the center and this will be used as the central circle of a medicine wheel constructed in the kiva for the first time. My grandmother felt this was essential. Access to the kiva is by means of a ladder reaching into the upper chamber, which pokes up four to five feet above ground. This architecture is the heart of Hopi cosmology."

He placed his hand on the medicine pouch at his belt that he had received from his grandmother when he was a young initiate into the mysteries. Manny paused for several minutes, as though he was listening to her voice before continuing the education of Tom.

"In the ceremonial chamber my grandmother has created a sand painting, using traditional symbols for animals, sea and lake creatures, corn seeds and plants, sky and earth. She has added new symbols for your spaceship and the new planet. You may understand now why she needs to know the precise location. You must inform her when you meet."

Tom leaned in closer to Manny so he did not miss a moment of the archetypal knowledge that was being shared. Manny explained that the four Sacred Keepers were unanimous in their enthusiasm for the interstellar venture.

Manny's grandmother was the Keeper of the Sky People and would be sitting at the North stone of the medicine wheel. She would track and find the energy passage to the new planet once she was provided with location specs.

The Keeper of the Animals was already gathering his essential energy to transport it through time and space. He would be at the East stone. The Keeper of Corn, Plants and Trees had spoken with these families and requested their co-operation, which was granted. That Sacred Keeper, an elderly woman elder, would sit at the South stone. The Keeper of the Earth would be located at the West stone for her to usher in the energy of new beginnings."

Tears ran down Manny's cheeks as he continued to realize the immensity of what the Hopi elders were offering.

"I will be at the fire pit right in the center of the chamber. My task is to keep the inside circle of the medicine wheel open so there is a portal for the energies to pour through to their new destination. The Sacred Keeper at the East stone will also concentrate on the spirit world energies to assist me. My grandmother called me in to do this, as I have been trained by her and have the spiritual strength to hold the portal open.

The four Sacred Keepers have specific energies to concentrate upon and send them through the portal."

The tears had not stopped as Manny said,

"The Keepers are elderly, all in their 80's, and I now realize that this ceremony is their last before departing this life."

They were both acutely silent, struck by this blow of terrifying dedication, taken aback that the Four Sacred Keepers were offering their lives to enable a renewal on a distant planet that none of them would experience.

Tom had to ask, "Manny, will you survive the ceremony?"

It was Manny's turn for silence. Eventually he answered slowly,

"No, I will not die in the sacred kiva, because I am coming with you to the new planet. You did get the instruction from my grandmother did you not?"

They both allowed a grim smile, but were overwhelmed by the intentions of the four elderly Sacred Keepers of the Hopi. The helicopter hovered over the dusty main plaza in Orobai, the only inhabited pueblo. The Hopi villages clung precariously to six hundred foot high escarpments looming out of the desert terrain, distributed on three rocky mesas.

The buildings in Orobai pueblo seemed almost surreal as they poked out of the desert surrounding the escarpment. Sunlight glinted on old pickup trucks, and barely into the remaining dwellings which were shuttered against the desert. Several horses could be seen tethered in a dusty compound.

They could see a gathering of people off to one side of the plaza where the helicopter put down to the north of the kiva. Orobai pueblo was the root of the annual cycle of ceremonies and this was where the remaining elders and their supporters now lived. The four Sacred Keepers were standing there wearing traditional garments: white tunics with dazzling Hopi woven blankets thrown over the shoulder. Their demeanor, calm and unworldly steadiness struck Tom forcibly as he looked over at the four incredible people who had offered to help his mission.

Tom was introduced to Manny's grandmother and the three other Sacred Keepers. They had dark wrinkled faces and they spoke to Manny in a deep guttural manner that felt as if it emanated from an ancient time, - which it did. He sensed their all-seeing wisdom and deep stillness. They had something about them that was outside of time and space and it cast an eerie presence that made Tom shiver in the heat of the desert.

When he looked into the eyes of Manny's grandmother, Tom sank down to his knees before her and wept, just as Manny had wept on the journey there. She calmly held out her hands to him and stood before him. He looked into the eyes of wisdom, beauty and power. She spoke to him in perfect English.

"I hope that Manny has instructed you well." She chuckled with that deep guttural sound he had heard before.

"You have the new planet's location for me?"

Tom nodded – there was nothing he could say.

She understood and said,

"We know what is to be created here and treat it as an honor to be part of it. It will be your task to place it in order on the new planet. I will introduce you to the other Keepers."

Tom was included in a circle of the most magnificent people he had ever met. The tears continued to flow down his face.

"This is good," remarked Manny's grandmother.

"Dr. Hagen, do not lament that we will not return from the kiva," she said. "I reassure you that this is what we want. We are ready to move on and become part of the Sky People. That is something all four of us have yearned for. We gladly reach for that transformation. We cannot invite you into the kiva. You must stay outside, next to where the North stone is placed. I will show you."

She took Tom by the hand and pointed out the chair placed right above the North stone in the subterranean chamber. Her smile was quite amused.

"We will be inside with the ceremony for the rest of the day. It will be completed by morning. You are to stay at this location throughout. Our people will bring you water and sustenance. At daybreak, Manny will come out by the ladder. There is a flat stone that fits the top of the kiva perfectly. You and Manny will place that over the entrance, as this kiva becomes our tomb, though it is only for our dead bodies. We will have gone elsewhere by dawn."

She looked deeply into Tom's eyes and he felt he was looking into universe after universe.

"I have one request. Do not ask Manny what took place in the ceremonial chamber of the kiva. When the time is right he will inform you. Until that time, please resist all curiosity about the Transfer Particle. The fact that you land safely on the new planet in the next galaxy is proof enough."

Tom relaxed for the first time, and said: "I now understand Manny's reference to your steel trap logic!"

She smiled again and he felt the deep love she extended to him and to all beings. She summoned her three companions and they nimbly climbed down the ladder into the womb of the Earth. Manny was the last to enter the kiva, pulling a wood and vine cover over the opening.

Tom took up his station at the North apex and for the first time in a long while he began to pray. He was not particularly spiritual but at that moment he became so. He remembered the chants and sutras from his flirtation with Buddhism much earlier in life, reflecting on the teachings of impermanence and emptiness. In that long night under the desert stars he internalized what he had ignored for so long. He knew that his contribution to the Four Sacred Keepers was stillness and the absence of thought.

He allowed his scientific mind to recede and felt deeply in his body the unification of universes. Tom opened up to the reality of something he had no prior knowledge of.

The taste of the burning fire pit at the center of the medicine wheel was pungent in his mouth.

Although the night was cold, beads of sweat broke out on his forehead and ran down his cheeks, splashing onto his buttoned shirt. He was starkly aware that the Sacred Keeper of the Sky People was directly below him. Manny's grandmother had given him specific instructions and he kept to them as though they were sacred vows.

He was in unfamiliar territory, which became more and more unusual as the night proceeded. Yet he was prepared to make that leap of faith to trust completely the elderly Hopi elders who were offering their lives.

Deep sobs arose in his chest and he cried uncontrollably several times during that long dark night. The first light of dawn on the desert horizon was not a relief, just a marker of the most significant act of his life.

The morning breeze raised a brief sand storm. He gripped the wood of the sturdy chair upon which he sat. He felt the knots of the hard wood with his two hands. This grounded him deeply in the experience of the four Sacred Keepers who he knew were now dead. Humbled by their nobility he waited patiently.

He made it through the rest of the night until he heard Manny's steps on the ladder and was there to embrace him as he climbed out of the sacred kiva. His new friend looked gaunt and bereft, yet had a steely determination in his eyes.

Between them, they lifted the stone slab and placed it on the opening of the kiva. They sat at the North apex where Tom had been stationed, very quiet, full of wonder and not a little grief.

Breakfast was brought over to them by the remaining elders of the pueblo, who knew what had taken place. The coffee was good, as were the corn tortillas. There was no need for any conversation or analysis.

Tom and Manny climbed into the helicopter and were quickly ferried to Phoenix International Airport.

It was a silent journey. Both men knew they had been radically changed.

Chapter Thirteen: The Forest

During my career as an anthropologist I was fortunate to encounter many First Nation story tellers across North America: Dene, Hopi, Ojibwa, Algonquin, Inuit – to mention a few. Their poetic recounting of myths and history had a deep impact on how I thought and wrote.

I would say that without poetry, cultures implode. In Chapter 10: Medicine Mentors, four extraordinary indigenous medicine people enhanced my process of remembering the power of the poetic voice. Through their mentoring, I learned how to reconfigure my understanding of time, place and consciousness. I chose to listen to the sacred feminine voice of Earth Wisdom rather than the multitude of competing voices in my deep unconscious.

So I made a radical turn in the 1980's to reconstruct anthropological methodology, as the poetic voice was always required for investigation of the cultural other.

I felt that the language of the anthropologist could not represent the raw experience of other cultures - therefore poetry was philosophically essential to the work of anthropology.

I saw poetry as an uninterrupted process whereas field notes were not. I suggested to colleagues that the poetry of observation is what anthropologists are supposed to be doing. Anthropologists who commit themselves to poetry in order to say something different about field experience are the tricksters and shamans of the discipline. I have been described as much worse!

The radicalization of the discipline and an evolution into a different kind of anthropology was required. A continuation of this perspective emerged several decades later when I brought out a personal volume of poetry in 2018 – *Painting with Words, Poetry for a New Era.*

The poems were split into six parts, each with its own distinctive theme. The final part is dedicated to Ancient Wisdom where an epic poem awaits the reader's attention. It was written when I accompanied two friends on the first leg of their cross Canada canoe expedition.

My good friend, Keith Crowe, teamed up with me and a yellow canoe. I had never undertaken anything quite like this. This long poem about Ancient Wisdom was written during the canoe trip, under oil skins, during portages, while cooking in the rain and once when standing drenched and half clothed in a Quebec laundromat.

My creation of this poem had a double focus. I wanted to leave a document about Canada's wilderness for my grand-children, so they could be inspired by Mother Earth.

When experience and inspiration sparked, I would shout out to Keith in the stern of the yellow canoe that I had to write. I would bring out the oil skin envelope stuffed with poems about the journey. I also wanted to weave in the Wisdom of the Elders, to speak about Canadian waterways from the reverence of First Nations, so that my grand-children would understand the meaning of rivers, forests and mountains.

The words "without poetry, cultures implode" require that I bring poetry to *Shattered Earth: Approaching Extinction,* as this leaves the door open for our species and leaders to change. I choose to complete this book with a moment from the prior focus on Ancient Wisdom. It pulsates with the rhythm of the river and the spirit of nature of its ancient inhabitants.

In this epic poem I criticize human greed and its destructive impulses that result in pollution, contamination and annihilation of the natural world. I am nostalgic for the ancient ways of the people who had held Mother Earth in sacred regard, so I take readers into the heart of nature's Zen-like serenity, and sheer "thereness."

The reader is hurled at the same time onto the path of nature's fury expressed through extreme weather conditions.

In spite of being exposed to the merciless harshness of the elements, the poet – that is me - still smiles because I am a part of this world, just like a tree or a rock.

I see Ancient Wisdom as the tabernacle of our collective memory, and I harvest these ancient energies and weave them into my own history.

In the poetry volume of 2018 I took the reader through the immensities of joy and pain, through the infinite and the mysterious. I dissect the dissonance of the modern world with the scalpel of poetic musings and describe the interflow between the human soul and the spirit of Earth - paving a quest for spiritual evolution and higher meaning.

I provide a poetic narrative of our basest attributes as a species, our greed and propensity toward a savage violence, as well as our ability to love beyond the telling power of words. Ancient Wisdom awakens the sense of the infinite within us, surging our hearts with the power of their message. My poetry aims directly for the heart, speaking to the reader in clear and loud words, sometimes screaming the truth. This restores the possibility of the ancient dialogue between humans and nature.

For *Shattered Earth:Approaching Extinction*, I take a portion of the epic poem in order to talk about The Forest. The connection between humans and nature is illustrated with a solitary tree and a man. In each other's presence, their feelings of aloneness vanish.

The Forest

Whisper of wind through pine needles.

Shimmering aspens and soft poplars of the forest.

Green – spring fresh green,

a relief to the year round darkness of the spruce's

darker timbre and twin pronged sheaths.

The river denies our passage

so we walk through sheltered forests

rather than meet

our death by foolishness.

We wander and find herbs, trilliums white in dense bush,

hiding among the wild strawberries

un-bodied with their

rich red summer promise.

Guardian trees, lichen laced,

protest the spring violets pushing upwards.

In the forest a great many entities

of the earth and sky speak of before

and what is to be.

Clearings sunk into the earth

await further visits.

In the center of one clearing

stood a single tall aspen

    -    lonely.

Waiting for companionship,

fragile in its aloneness,

in her aloneness,

in our aloneness.

I stand within her circle

    -    this tree and I -

and for a brief moment,

neither were alone.

ABOUT THE AUTHOR'S WORKS

Shattered Earth: Approaching Extinction is my 18th book – the most difficult yet. It is about our broken world – particularly with respect to the impending Extinction brought about by Climate Emergency. The difficulty for me has been the darkness of Extinction despite the pacifying alternative of Impermanence. Yet my prior writing of 17 books has brought this steadily my way to write a candid document about *Shattered Earth.*

I Had a Dream

I dreamed I was in a river running kayak, sitting quietly in a pool outside the swift eddies racing to the edge of a waterfall that was huge, sheer, with a vertical drop of 1,000 feet. The kayak was bright yellow, the short stubby craft an extension of my body. My wetsuit was black and I wore a red lifejacket tightly fastened. My helmet was also red. The shaft of the paddle was black, the twin blades a dancing red.

I looked around at the high mountains and forest, noticing the mist rising from the swift flowing river. Then pushed the kayak into the racing eddies straight to the edge of the waterfall. As I went over, I raised the paddle high over my head and leaned back. I did nothing to steer or guide the kayak.

The descent seemed forever - timeless. Yet in a moment my craft had submerged into the river below and then I was bobbing on the surface paddling downstream. My first thought in the dream as I manoeuvred close to the river's edge was "That was a really bad run. I didn't do anything."

Then moments later in the dream I stopped my thinking, realizing that it was the perfect run, precisely because I did not interfere with forces greater than mine. I had missed the significance of surrender to the fierce current of the waterfall, to the awesome power of the stream of consciousness which was far more important.

The dream lingered in my mind long enough to reveal that my literary works were the stream of consciousness - just different pearls on the same thread.

I had flown into the small airport of Castlegar in the Kootenay Mountains of British Columbia for my son's wedding in the summer of 2009. The short hop over the Rockies in a Dash 8 aircraft from Calgary was spectacular, especially the flight into Castlegar airport.

The wingtips seemed to touch the valley mountains, as the aircraft swerved sharply into the river fringed village of Castlegar. My son Iain, his bride to be – Nancy – and my grandson Callun were there to deliver me to where I was staying that night in nearby Nelson. The wedding ceremony was the next day in the Tibetan Buddhist Gompa.

The unforgettable dream, vivid in every detail, took place that evening in Nelson. I shared this dream with Iain and Nancy next morning, so they could perhaps see for themselves the surrender to the other, necessary for their marriage to mature well.

They understood. Their dharma and mountain friends enjoyed an incredible wedding in the Tibetan Gompa. There was a mountain of alcohol at the reception and dance afterwards, bottles of wine, beer and whisky with a line of glasses for Mai Tais. Yet hardly anyone drank, as the "high" was the quality of celebration and surrender in the wedding ceremony.

I have thought about this dream a great deal over the past decades and the reflections were most revealing. Where was it taking me? I eventually realized it was into the dark space of Extinction of our species. That was the shock that went through me.

To the best of my ability, I endeavor to follow Gandhi's principles of *ahimsa* (do not harm) and the teachings on mindfulness. These are the guidelines and foundations for my peace and environmental activism. I live very simply as a planetary activist, Zen teacher, and recognized guru in India.

My initial task is to refine my own consciousness - to be a vehicle to chart an authentic path. If I did not do this, I could not write *Shattered Earth: Approaching Extinction*.

The focus on daily mindfulness enables me to be still and clear. Steadiness, clarity and compassion are there, rather than ego posturing from the lunatic fringe.

Though there was a "rush" from the latter, I prefer the still-point, uncoloured by the excess of ego and desire for recognition. It propels me to serve the planet and humanity by creating bridges and pathways of mindfulness for community activism.

The creation of my 2008 book – *Failsafe: Saving the Earth from Ourselves* – was part of this process though I did not realize it at the time. It was written from an unusual place and was also the midpoint for two trilogies of books.

Many years ago prior to the beginning of spring after a severe winter in Canada, I participated in a sweat lodge ceremony with respected elders from the Ojibwa, Dene and Mohawk First Nations. We made deeply personal and collective commitments to serve the Earth Mother.

At the end of the ceremony we emerged into the pristine beauty of a late snowfall under a clear star studded sky. There had been a two-inch snowfall during the ceremony.

As we walked barefoot to where we were camping I turned round and saw our footprints in the snow.

It seemed as though these were the first footprints on the new Earth. I gestured to my companions to stop and look.

They silently shared the same insight with soft smiles. In that instant the stillness and silence renewed our commitments to serve Mother Earth with all our hearts and minds. That was the moment when I became integrated with the Wisdom of the Elders.

Failsafe was born from that moment at the end of winter in 2006. It was published in October 2008. I was giving a talk about this experience to an audience in Vancouver and suddenly found myself talking about two previous books I had published and the next three books not yet written.

Failsafe was the midpoint. All these books were writing me, although I was not aware of it. Each book had issued forth from the experience of profound silence. A life work writing me! It took me years to wake up to this. The first book in this trilogy - *Anthropology at The Edge* - was published in 1997, followed by *The Essential Spiral* in 2002 and *Failsafe* in 2008. My insights, disasters and occasional breakthroughs were the basis for this abundance.

These books were university text books and the basis for two television courses. They investigated the necessity of changing the mindset of humanity in order to combat Climate Change.

I knew that if we continue to turn our beautiful rivers into sewers because of our endless greed and neglected ignorance, there is no place on Mother Earth to sustain our present civilization. It will join the trash heap collectively created by mindless generations of humanity.

We have allowed the environment to become an extension of human egocentric needs and values – an ego-sphere rather than an eco-sphere. In this ego-sphere we consume mindlessly in the global economy without regard for ecosystem balance or our creation of vast inequality and poverty.

Planetary care is not part of this agenda. I wrote about *homo sapiens* as a Failed Genetic Experiment, though did place a question mark after "Experiment."

My deepest hope, however, was that our innate knowledge would somehow become manifest, as we interconnect with a vast counter culture that is no longer a minority, no longer asleep or disempowered.

Diligent mindfulness can change our brain structures in the direction that permits new paradigms of behavior to come into form. As cells in the ecosystem of Gaia, humanity can align their neuronal networks with principles of ecosystem balance, ethics and responsibility.

The plan in my mind was that the critical mass would arrive and amount to a collective tipping point for our species. Once the ego-driven mind is reined in, then clarity and compassion are suddenly there to provide the basis for how we can be with the planet and with one another in a totally new way.

This is what happens if we "Begin It Now" – the concluding words to *Failsafe: Saving the Earth From Ourselves.*

The following book – *Earth My Body, Water My Blood* – was co-authored with students in my university class on Ecology and Culture.

The students brought passion, insight and sheer hard work to investigate the basic components of a new social and economic form for the 21st century – eco-community.

It was based on the Five Great Elements – Earth, Water, Air, Fire and Space – inherent in all aspects of life.

The driving force adopted by the students was from the feminine representation of enlightenment.

I have always thought of the present millennium as the century of the daughters. Not so much as a gender separate phenomenon, but as attributes of a holistic, nurturing presence of mind. These principles have parallels with Vedic philosophy and are found in Indigenous, Chinese and Western Alchemical traditions.

Circles within circles all interconnecting – beautifully expressed by the Oglala Sioux medicine man, Black Elk, as the interdependent hoops of all nations and traditions.

The students had decided on a profound template for this collection. Their adventure to establish eco-communities reflected the shift in mindset required to salvage the global ecosystem for human habitation.

Our present values and patterns are the architects of the present global ecological emergency.

We are our environment. Whether we live in a rural or urban locale, in the industrial or developing worlds, our mindset has to be focused on living as one component of Gaia's ecosystem.

The second trilogy after *Failsafe* begins with *Redemption*. It was a lost manuscript, first written in 1975. I rediscovered this heartfelt book in 2011.

The narrative was vivified with hindsight from my writer's eye years later.

The story is an allegory for life difficulties I experienced at that time. I was a real mess, yet despite my desperate state of mind this novel about Awakening emerged.

Laced with grim humor, the novel has nature's harsh and beautiful rhapsody as the background for tragic human failings.

Redemption is set in The Hebrides, islands off the northwest coast of Scotland, with startling cycles of maturing and downfall of the epic character, Callum Mor. He was a gifted child, master mariner and derelict drunk, who eventually gains wisdom from a hard life's journey.

Redemption reads like an extended prose poem reflecting the primal forces of nature and of human nature. The starkly gorgeous and remote island setting creates and reinforces the central themes of struggle, family, community and wonder at the beauty of the world.

Redemption alludes to more than what is openly stated.

The scenes provide a striking visual clarity that draw on the realm of timeless storytelling. This rattles the tapestry to find deeper messages of compassion and faith to emerge.

Book Two of the trilogy, *Trailing Sky Six Feathers, One Man's Journey with His Muse* is a Hero's Journey - as if Indiana Jones meets the Buddha with a dash of Celestine Prophecy.

Shamanic healing of childhood sexual abuse, guru training and near death experience in an Indian ashram has this author stumbling through the first part of life, then standing strong in his own sovereignty in the latter part. Past life memories collide head on with the present.

With a voice steeped in authentic experience, I navigate past and present lives over four centuries; from brutal raids on Indian settlements in 18th century Arizona, insane sea voyages off the Scottish Hebrides in the 20th century, to a decisive life moment of surrender to the Muse in the 21st century.

These epic tales weave seamlessly to create inspiration for a wide range of fellow spiritual seekers. The genre is legend mixed with autobiography.

In *New Planet, New World,* I bring the 18th century to collide with the 21st century. Time, culture, space and consciousness are fused across centuries to create the final book of this trilogy.

New Planet, New World provides a counterpoint to the demise of modern civilization. I chart a Beginning Anew for humanity, a communal Hero's Journey to reconstruct society based on ecology, caring and sharing, as power elites ignore their complicity in the destruction of life on Planet Earth.

This adventure is not without risk or cost. The dark episodes and lyrical passages move the story along with action, fear, resolution, death, bravery and exile in a futuristic opportunity for humanity.

This action-packed book of intertwining plotlines arc into the epiphany of the final chapter, which muses about human survival anywhere. This end game is a philosophy for the future.

The reader now begins to harken to the rip tides of this futuristic novel and can anticipate just where I am going!

My career as an anthropologist took me to First Nation story tellers.

This prompted me to rethink the purpose of field work, convinced that it lacked the poetic voice that I had heard from the story tellers. To prove this, I called on forty brilliant anthropologists, many of them senior icons in the discipline, to send me the poems they wrote while studying the cultural other.

Much to my surprise the American Anthropological Association (AAA) published the ensuing book I edited.

In 1985 *Reflections: The Anthropological Muse* was released by the AAA at their annual conference and held up as a new direction for the next century of anthropology. Here's why:

My basic contention, shared by many other anthropologists, was that something crucial was missing from field work. The study of other cultures had often become pseudo-forms, which were neither true to the cultural other or to the science of anthropology.

I proposed a poetry of observation in order to close the epistemological gap between observer and cultural other. In this way the poetic dimension became a crucial part of the developing methodology of anthropology. It had the function of revealing what has been suppressed and ignored.

I wanted a different kind of anthropology, one that would engage dialectically with the cultural other and express it in a way that is useful for the other culture and my own society.

Reflections: The Anthropological Muse changed the manner in which anthropology is justified and practiced.

A continuation of this radical perspective emerged three decades later when I brought out a personal volume of poetry in 2018 – *Painting with Words Poetry for a New Era.* Some words from a Five Star Review may bring that piece of the thread home.

Kathryn Bennet, an American poet, wrote:

"I read this book three times before settling in to write this review. Each time I felt that I uncovered another layer with the collection of poems that I had missed the last time through. To me there is something truly magical about a work that can do that… The poems strike right at the heart of the journey the author himself has taken in life, and yet it also has an ability to resound with others… You can see the images come to life before your eyes as you read… This collection of poems takes the reader through the full gamut of human emotions. The author has masterfully used his own life experience to transport the reader through this journey, while striving to leave a mark directly on the reader's heart."

I also brought out four e books on Buddhist Dharma and placed them on Amazon Kindle, *Keeping Dharma Alive* Volume 1 & 2; *Portals and Passages* Book 1 & 2.

I was assessing this path as a way to handle the incoming extinction I felt was so imminent, so placed dharma and environment in sync with one another. In my television course on Ecology and Environment I presented the Five Mindfulness Trainings from Buddhism as being nothing other than Environmental Ethics.

Our World Is Burning, My Views on Mindful Engagement soon followed. The sixteen essays offered examples of how to respond to the most serious social, economic, environmental and personal challenges of the 21st century.

I thought Mindful Engagement would be a tenable tool to cultivate awareness as an ethical framework which would guide actions, create steadiness and equanimity, and furthermore replenish body, mind and spirit. The book was offered as a lightning bolt to singe incredulity and cynicism.

Charting an Authentic Path

This review of my books reinforces the attempt to create an authentic tapestry about the state of our world. This is what everyone wants to do if they only just stop and think about it. It is a natural response to all the inauthenticity that surrounds us daily.

This present time needs a still-point that permits us to create bridges and pathways of harmony. From this energy - change, poems, chapters and books emerge.

My writing delivers a vigorous message about personal transformation in order to become different stewards of the earth and society.

In the Sixteen Essays of *Our World is Burning*, I offer reality-based information that is in high demand in today's society, which provides the potential for my projects to become fresh, new icons for today's hungry culture. Hungry, that is, for authentic transformation.

It takes training, practice, intelligence and creative vision to find the drive to create a tangible spirit of co-operation, the willingness to share and be supportive, and learning how to cross the bridges of conflict. This thread of understanding finds a place in every essay in *Our World is Burning*.

The global movement towards mindful engagement in all spheres of life is meeting with gradual success, which in turn has fueled this work.

The modern "fear of missing out" generation prods me to "Up My Game", as it were, and steadily examine the Darkness and Extinction that is rapidly drawing closer to wiping humanity from this planet.

In this present work – *Shattered Earth* - I develop a perspective to handle Extinction well - though I do find it difficult to write about Darkness and Extinction.

So, I draw on sages, Wisdom of the Elders and attempt to face Extinction with bravery and a developed consciousness. I am encouraged by a quote from Thich Nhat Hanh;

> *"Someone asked me, "Aren't you worried about the state of the world?" I allowed myself to breathe and then I said, "What is most important is not to allow your anxiety about what happens to fill your heart. If your heart is filled with anxiety, you will get sick, and you will not be able to help."*

This takes me to recognize the significance of impermanence, which could be deemed a pacifying response to ecological apocalypse and the Sixth Extinction.

Protest and rebellion to any nation's inadequate attempts about Climate Change are unlikely to succeed. They may be thought of as the alternative to impermanence - but they will certainly be brutally dispersed by national police and military.

Thus the outcome of Extinction remains almost unstoppable before our eyes.

I return to the dream of the waterfall with a vertical drop of 1,000 feet. This was where I surrendered to the awesome stream of consciousness pouring through me and the books I write.

The beginning of a long journey - and one body of work culminates in my writing about *Shattered Earth: Approaching Extinction.*

About The Author

Poet, Global Traveler, Founder of Friends for Peace, Guru in India, Zen teacher and Spiritual Warrior for planetary care, peace and social justice.

Ian Prattis presently lives in Ottawa, Canada and encourages people to find their true nature, so that humanity and the planet may be renewed. He mostly stays local to help turn the tide in his home city so that good things begin to happen spontaneously.

Dr. Ian Prattis is Professor Emeritus at Carleton University in Ottawa, Canada. He is an award winning author of seventeen books. Recent awards include Gold for *Redemption* at the 2015 Florida Book Festival, 2015 Quill Award from Focus on Women Magazine for *Trailing Sky Six Feathers* and Silver for Environment from the 2014 Living Now Literary Awards for *Failsafe; Saving the Earth From Ourselves.*

His novel – *Redemption* – is being made into a movie. His poetry, memoirs, fiction, articles, blogs and podcasts appear in a wide range of venues.

He was born in the UK and has spent much of his life living and teaching in Canada.

His moving and eye-opening books and poetry are a memorable experience for anyone who enjoys reading about primordial tendencies.

Beneath the polished urban facade remains a part of human nature that few want to acknowledge, either due to fear or simply because it is easier to deny the basic instincts that have kept us alive on an unforgiving earth. Prattis bravely goes there in his outstanding literary work. A stone tossed into the waters of life.

Born on October 16, 1942, in Great Britain, Ian grew up in Corby, a tough steel town populated by Scots in the heartland of England's countryside.

Cultural interface was an early and continuing influence. Ian was an outstanding athlete and scholar at school, graduating with distinctions in all subjects. He did not stay to collect graduating honours, as at seventeen years old he travelled to Sarawak, Borneo, with Voluntary Service Overseas (1960 – 62), Britain's Peace Corps.

He loved the immersion in the myriad cultures of Sarawak and was greatly amused by the British colonial mentality, which he did not share. He worked in a variety of youth programs as a community development officer, and also explored the headwaters of Sarawak's major rivers, with expeditions into Indonesian Borneo.

Returning to Great Britain after Sarawak was an uneasy transition. He did, however, manage to stumble through an undergraduate degree in anthropology at University College, London (1962 – 65), before continuing with graduate studies at Balliol College, Oxford (1965 – 67).

At Oxford, academics took a back seat to the judo dojo, rugby field, bridge table, and the founding of irreverent societies at Balliol. Yet by the time he pursued doctoral studies at the University of British Columbia (1967 – 70), his brain switched on. He renewed his passion for other cultures, placing his research on North West Coast fishing communities within a mathematical, experimental domain that the discipline of anthropology was not quite ready for. Being at the edge of new endeavours was natural to him, and continues to be so.

He was Professor of Anthropology and Religion at Carleton University from 1970 to 2007. He has worked with diverse groups all over the world and has a passion for doing anthropology. His career trajectory has curved through mathematical models, development studies, hermeneutics, poetics and symbolic anthropology, to new science and consciousness studies. The intent was always to expand across existing boundaries, to renew the freshness of the anthropological endeavour and make the discipline relevant to the individuals and cultures it touches.

He studied Tibetan Buddhism with Lama Tarchin in the early 1980's, Engaged Buddhism with Zen Master Thich Nhat Hanh much later, Christian meditation with the Benedictines, and was trained by First Nation medicine people and shamans in their healing practices. He also studied the Vedic tradition of Siddha Samadhi Yoga, and taught this tradition of meditation in India. He was ordained as a teacher and initiator – the first westerner to receive this privilege – and is acknowledged in India as a guru.

Later in life he lived in a hermitage in Kingsmere, Quebec, in the middle of Gatineau Park forest when his pet wolf was alive. He facilitated a meditation community in Ottawa called the Pine Gate Mindfulness Community from 1997 to 2017. At the outbreak of the Iraq war he founded Friends for Peace Canada – a coalition of meditation, peace, activist and environmental groups to work for peace, planetary care and social justice.

He received the 2011 Ottawa Earth Day Environment Award and edits an online Buddhist Journal. In 2018 he received the Yellow Lotus Award from the Vesak Project for his spiritual guidance and teaching of the Dharma. Since retiring from Carleton University in 2007 he has authored four e-books on dharma, seven books and this poetry volume.

He enjoys the freedom to create at his own pace and has yet to discern the meaning of retirement.

Manor House
905-648-2193
www.manor-house-publishing.com